To

Bill Lawson

my colleague in
ministry

with appreciation
for our year together

and with great expe-
tations for his
future ministry

Warmly in Christ,
Bob Hudnut

5/28/76

CHURCH GROWTH
IS NOT THE POINT

BY ROBERT K. HUDNUT

THE SLEEPING GIANT

AROUSING THE SLEEPING GIANT

AN ACTIVE MAN AND THE CHRIST

A SENSITIVE MAN AND THE CHRIST

A THINKING MAN AND THE CHRIST

SURPRISED BY GOD

CHURCH GROWTH IS NOT THE POINT

CHURCH GROWTH IS NOT THE POINT

ROBERT K. HUDNUT

HARPER & ROW, PUBLISHERS

New York, Evanston, San Francisco, London

Designed by Janice Stern

Library of Congress Cataloging in Publication Data

Hudnut, Robert K
   Church growth is not the point.

   Incudes bibliographical references.
   1. Christianity—20th century. 2. Church membership. 3. Christian life—Presbyterian authors.
I. Title.
BR121.2.H77   260   74–25692
ISBN 0–06–064062–6

75 76 77 78 79 10 9 8 7 6 5 4 3 2

To all the people in churches
  from Clearwater, Florida
  to Los Angeles, California
who have invited me to share
  the deep places with them
and reminded me that church growth
  is not the point,
faithfulness to the Gospel is

Behold, like the clay in the potter's hand,
so are you in my hand, O house of Israel.

JEREMIAH 18:6

I will not . . . speak of anything except what
Christ has wrought through me.

ROMANS 15:18

It is no longer I who live, but Christ who
lives in me.

GALATIANS 2:20

Paul, a slave of Jesus Christ.

ROMANS 1:1

I am nothing.

2 CORINTHIANS 12:11

CONTENTS

PREFACE

It is a tough time for the American church. In many quarters membership is down. Attendance is down.

But church growth is not the point. The point is whether the church is being true to the Gospel. And, in city after city and town after town, it is. Indeed, *because* it is being faithful it is often *losing* members.

There are men and women serving pulpits all over America who refuse to huckster Christ, who are dead serious about the claims the Suffering Servant makes upon them, who will not give an inch when a well-heeled church member says in an official board meeting, "You give our church's money to _____, and I'm leaving the church."

Loss of growth in statistics has often meant increase in growth in the Gospel. The "dead wood" is gone. The "faithful remnant" remains. The church is lean and stripped for action in the '70s.

These are the people for whom this book is written—the people who are still slogging it out in the Sunday School, who still come to choir rehearsal once a week, who are in the pews on Sunday morning giving the minister or pastor or priest all the support in the world.

They are the people who know that something is there. No, it may not be the greatest show in town. Yes, one or two heads may nod. The choir may be flat and the children may come home confused between Noah's Ark and the Ark of the Covenant.

But the people are there because God is there. No, not necessarily. Not inevitably. Certainly not just because it is a church. But possibly. Often. Sometimes, yes, dramatically. After all, it was in an average "church service" that Isaiah heard God speak.

God *is* what keeps us hanging in there at the corner of State and Main. Waiting. Catching the fire. Being gripped by the most powerful force in the world. Committed to turn the world upside down (Acts 17:6). Turning it.

That's what doing church in the 1970s is all about. And that's why millions of people every week, in decreasing numbers but increasing power, are saying, "Church growth is not the point. Faithfulness to our Lord Jesus Christ is."

Here's a book on how to be faithful. Correction: on how God, incredibly, is being faithful through us—good old middle-class, statistically faltering, us.

This means, among other things, the recovery of the passive. The passive is the agent of the Holy Spirit. It is no accident that the Holy Spirit is playing such a vital part in the renewal of churches today. We do not choose to become church members. We *are* chosen. We do not choose to go the second mile. We *are* ordered. And, as slaves, the most popular way of referring to Christians in the first-century church, we *find* ourselves obeying.

The de-emphasis on church growth also means a reemphasis on the Old Testament. One of the reasons the church in recent years has been so wide of the mark is that it has lost its historic roots. It is probably safe to say that less than a fifth of the sermons preached in churches today are from the Old Testament. We have lost the awesome dimension of confrontation, of God coming at us all the time, of his commands, his provocations, his insults. It is time to recover our feel for Moses, Isaiah, Jeremiah, Ezekiel, Hannah, and countless others in our tradition who found that, out of those confrontations, incredible things were being done through them.

It is those same things—unbelievable but somehow not undo-able—that are happening in church after dwindling church across the face of America. A building fund is being matched by a benevolence fund. That is a guaranteed way to *lose* church members and *grow* as a church! A commitment is made by the church's official board to match every dollar of "operating" with a dollar to "benevolences." That will alienate every white, Anglo-Saxon Protestant American who says, "Charity begins at home."

People are leaving the church. It could not be a better sign. Indeed, while they are leaving church income is growing. It was up 5.2 percent in 1973, according to the National Council of Churches. This proves that, the more serious the membership, the more substantial the church. As I have indicated in this book's two predecessors, *The Sleeping Giant* and *Arousing the Sleeping Giant,* most churches could be two-thirds smaller and lose nothing in power. In most churches, the first third are committed, the second third are peripheral, and the third third are out.

This book is written for all those who have been concerned about "the drop in church membership," and who now see in it a grace-filled, spirit-charged opportunity to "turn the world upside down" for Jesus Christ.

1

THE LOCAL CHURCH'S INABILITY
TO DO ANYTHING

I

Obviously a church does everything it can. It draws up a plan. It will emphasize this. It will deemphasize that. And much of what it plans it will do. It is an active church. It plans its activity. And what it says it will do it does.

The church members study (Acts 2:42). They share (Acts 2:42). They serve (John 12:26). They think. They feel. They act. They leave out nothing in their plan for exploring the transcendent. "Work out your own salvation" (Phil. 2:12), said St. Paul. And an active church does.

Turn the other cheek. Go the second mile. Sell what you have and give to the poor. Love your enemies. Love your neighbor. Love your God.

> *If* you do not forgive men their trespasses, neither will your Father forgive your trespasses (Matt. 6:15).

It was clearly conditional—no action in the fourth dimension, no progress.

> *If* you will obey my voice and keep my covenant, you shall be my own possession (Exod. 19:5).

What if you don't obey? "Clearly conditional," says an expert.[1] No action, no progress.

> *If* you obey . . . then you shall live   (Deut. 30:16).

It couldn't be clearer. Action is demanded.

> But if your heart turns away . . . you shall perish   (Deut. 30:17–18).

It was explicit.

> The Lord . . . keeps covenant . . . with *those who love him* . . . and requites . . . those who hate him   (Deut. 7:9–10).

That sums it up for the Old Testament.

> Every one *who believes in him* receives forgiveness of sins (Acts 10:43).

That sums it up for the New. No belief—no forgiveness. No action—no progress. No work—no faith. No faith—no grace.

The thief on the cross did confess his faith. The Prodigal Son did come back. The laborers did work one hour. Zaccheus did climb the tree. "What shall we *do?*" they asked Peter (Acts 2:37). "Repent," he said. "Repent," Jesus said (Mark 1:15). No repentance—no progress. No work—no faith. No faith—no grace. "Repentance and amendment," summarizes another expert, "are the *conditions of* salvation."[2]

II

But are they? Yes, according to much of the Bible. But no, according to much more of the Bible. No matter how hard a church works, says the Bible's other strand, it is not going to make it in the religious dimension. Nor is the individual church member. You are not going to turn the other cheek. You are not going to go the second mile. You are not going to sell what you have and give to the poor. And you are not going to love your neighbor. Let alone your enemy. Let alone God. You are not going to forgive. You are not going to obey. You are not going to believe. You are not going to repent. You are not going to study, share, or serve.

They are impossible expectations. That does not mean they are not valuable. It only means they are not possible. Indeed, their value lies precisely in their impossibility. "With men it *is* impossible," Jesus said immediately after telling the rich man to sell what he had and give to the poor (Mark 10:27). "But not with God," he added. "All things are possible with God." That was the point. "Work out your own salvation, for *God* is at work in you." That was the point.

Yes, the works are important. To show failure. To show the limits of the active. To show the limits of "growth." To throw a church onto the passive. To throw it onto God. God *is* what makes an active church passive. God *is* what makes an active church fail. God *is* what makes an active church realize *it is not its own doing.* "By grace you have been saved through faith; and this is *not* your own doing, it is the gift of God—not because of works, lest any man should boast. For we are his workmanship" (Eph. 2:8–9).

Note the passive. We have *been* saved. It is not our doing. It is a gift. It is not because of works. We are his workmanship. Grace is a gift, not a goal. There is *nothing* church members can do to get grace except realize that *they* cannot get it. The only point of the work is to see that the work doesn't work. We fail at politics. We fail at community action. We fail at our jobs. We fail at our churches. We fail at our homes. The point of the work is that the work doesn't work. Grace is a gift not a goal. An active church does all that it can. Then it is thrown onto God. Then it becomes passive. "This is not your own doing."

Less acting is called for in churches, more being acted on. Fewer potters, more clay. Less activity, more passivity. Less doing it, more letting it be done to us. "I am he who causes to happen what happens," God said (see Exod. 3:14). We let God happen rather than make God happen. We are passive. There can be a new birth of the spirit in churches. It is a matter not of church members' ability but of their inability, not of our success but of our failure, not of our being goal-oriented but gift-oriented. It is a matter not of the Pharisee, who says I can, but of the disciple, who says I can't. It is a matter not of the active church, which says we do, but of the passive church, which says let it be done to us. It is not our own doing. "I am nothing" (2 Cor: 12:11), Paul said.

*

Your activity as a church got you nowhere except to show you that your activity got you nowhere, which was certainly helpful, but you didn't even need that. Look what happened to Paul. Furiously active, doing all the right things to get to God, studying, sharing, serving, and farther from God than ever. Then God happened. The high achiever found that he had achieved nothing. The immensely successful professional found that he had succeeded at nothing. It was only when the doer became the done-to, that he made any progress in his religion. It was only when things began to be done *through* him rather than *by* him. "This is not your own doing."

Why do we limit ourselves to what can be done by us as activists rather than through us as churches? That's why the statistics are off. That's what causes the concern. Because we are pharisees when we should be disciples. We have to have the credit. We have to get in on the act. We have to do it. But the Bible is the book of the passive, not of what people have done but of what has been done through them. We have done nothing except, like Paul, realize we could do nothing. That's why church growth is off. People can't stand the passive.

Can anyone in a church tithe? Of course not. It is done through us, not by us. Can anyone turn the other cheek, go the second mile, love the enemy? Of course not. Even when approximations occur, they are done through us not by us. "*Not* because of works. . . . We are his workmanship." "It is not your own doing." "You did not choose me," Jesus said, "but I chose you" (John 15:16). The first church members did nothing to deserve being chosen. A businessman. An accountant. A man who worked for the IRS. They had no track record, and he chose them. "I chose you." "It is not your own doing." "By the grace of God I am what I am," Paul wrote. "I *worked* harder than any of them, though *it was not I*, but the grace of God which is with me" (1 Cor. 15:10).

*

Adam and Eve. "Let us make man in our image" (Gen: 1.26). "God formed man" (Gen. 2:7). "The Lord God took the man" (Gen. 2:15). The passive begins in the first story. It was the point of the story: that they refused to be passive. They were as pharisaical, as Promethean, as active, as goal-oriented as the rest of us.

Noah. "God said to Noah" (Gen. 6:13). "God remembered Noah" (Gen. 8:1). "God blessed Noah" (Gen. 9:1).

Abraham. "The Lord said to Abram, 'Go' " (Gen. 12:1). "And I will make of you a great nation, and I will bless you" (Gen. 12:2).

Moses. "God called to him out of the bush" (Exod. 3:4). "And the Lord said to Moses" (Exod. 4:21). "The Lord saved Israel" (Exod. 14:30).

The point of the Bible is that there is an entire dimension to life which we have not begun to explore, which we have not let explore *us*, the dimension of the passive, of what can be done through us rather than by us. That is the transcendent.

> I chose David (1 Kings 8:16).
> I chose Israel (Ezek. 20:5).
> He chose us (Eph. 1:4).
> He appeared to me (1 Cor. 15:8).

> Christ Jesus has made me his own (Phil. 3:12).
> You are not your own (1 Cor. 6:19).
> This is not your own doing (Eph. 2:8).

*

Yes, it's an insult to active church people. That's why they quit. But so what? It may be the only way we will ever become passive. To have our work denied. To have it scorned. To have it add up to nothing. To have been busy all our church lives doing nothing. "We have *nothing* to do with our own salvation," summarizes William Barclay.[3] "Neither he who plants," wrote Paul, "nor he who waters is *anything*, but only *God* who gives the growth" (1 Cor. 3:7).

No, you don't even have to repent. Paul didn't. He was on his way to haul Christians to jail when it happened. He didn't do anything. Indeed, everything he was doing was the wrong thing. He wouldn't even let it happen. But it happened. "I am he who causes to happen what happens." "This is not your doing." "With men it is impossible."

> Almighty God, who doth freely pardon all who repent and turn to Christ.

No. That is not the point at all.

> Almighty God, who doth freely pardon all.

That is the point. That is the announcement. That is the insult, the stumbling block, the folly (1 Cor. 1:23). And that is the new version of a major denomination's book of worship.

> I declare to you, in the name of Jesus Christ, we *are* forgiven.

That's the gospel. That's the fourth dimension. That's the passive. "We are forgiven," and there is nothing we can do about it except accept or reject the announcement, be passive, in other words, or active. "You did not choose me, but I chose you." "This is not your doing."

> I have been *crucified* with Christ; it is *no longer I who live,* but Christ who lives in me; . . . who loved *me* and gave himself for *me* (Gal. 2:20).

> We love, because he *first* loved us (1 John 4:19).

*

Yes, the thief on the cross confessed his faith, but it was in response to the man beside him. Yes, the Prodigal Son came back, but it was in response to his father's love. Yes, the laborers in the vineyard worked one hour, but it was in response to the man who gave them the job. Yes, Zaccheus climbed the tree, but it was in response to the man entering town. "Faith," Luther said, "is our response to God's grace." You can't believe your way to God. You believe your way *from* God. You can't work your way to God. You work your way *from* God. Grace is what happens. Faith is letting it happen *to* you. Works are letting it happen *through* you.

"You did not choose me, but I chose you." Precisely. The Bible was there with its announcement before we were there with our need. When we as church members came to Jesus, it was *after* he had come to us—through the Bible, the parents, the church, the church school. We came in response to news. We chose in response to choice. We worked in response to faith. We believed in response to grace.

It is *then* that we are driven to the passive action of repentance. You do not repent your way to God; you repent your way from God. God is not a goal but a gift.

> Woe is me! [cried Isaiah] for I am a man of unclean lips (Isa. 6:5).

It happened *after* God had happened.

> I am nothing [Paul confessed] (2 Cor. 12:11).

It happened *after* Jesus had happened.

> The Lord your God has chosen *you* (Deut. 7:6).

It happened *after* the Exodus had happened.

> It was *not* because you were more in number than any other people (Deut. 7:7).

No condition. No repentance. No work. No action.

> But it is because the Lord *loves* you (Deut. 7:8).

It is the acme of the passive, and it comes *before* the injunction to love him back (Deut. 7:9).[4]

*

It is also the acme of action. The passive is where the action is. We have not begun to experience the action of the passive in our churches. We have been too busy trying to make God happen when we should have relaxed and let God happen. You cannot study, share, and serve your way to God. You can only study, share, and serve your way from God. First the announcement, then the response. First the grace, then the faith. First the event, then the act.

It is the passive actions that are the powerful ones. We have failed for the most part as churches. We have been active, but we have not been passive, not nearly enough. We have wanted it to be done *by* us rather than *through* us. We have wanted to put conditions on grace rather than let grace put conditions on us.

We have struggled for the goal but been embarrassed by the gift. We have put growth of the church ahead of growth in the gospel.

It is time for the church to do the passive acts of servanthood. Correction: it is time for the passive acts of servanthood to be done through the churches. It may well mean the opposite of "growth." The servant is the symbol of the passive. Everything is done to him and through him. *Nothing* is done by him. The first church members called themselves servants (Rom. 1:1, Jude 1, *et pas*). They did only passive acts. Correction: passive acts *were* done *through* them. That was what it meant to be a *church*. The passive act of repentance, yes. The passive act of prayer. The passive act of witness. The passive act of healing. The passive act of first-century worship. The passive act of silence. The passive act of crucifixion. The ultimate passive act of the resurrection and victory over death.

It is *then* that the power which has eluded us as churches will come. We will be passive. We will do all that we can that is not our own doing. We will become his workmanship. The church members who are left will be able to say with Paul: "I will not venture to speak of anything except what *Christ* has wrought *through* me" (Rom. 15:18). And with the unknown Christian: "By grace you have been saved through faith; and this is *not* your own doing, it is the *gift* of *God.*"

NOTES

1. Samuel Terrien, *Job: The Poet of Existence* (Indianapolis: Bobbs-Merrill, 1957), p. 67.
2. Alan Richardson in *The Interpreter's Dictionary of the Bible* (New York: Abingdon, 1962), vol. 4, p. 178, ital. add.
3. Wm. Barclay, *The Letters to the Galatians and Ephesians* (Phila.: Westminster, 1958), p. 121, ital. add.
4. *V. sup.*, p. 2.

2

THE LOCAL CHURCH'S ABILITY
TO DO EVERYTHING

There are some excellent objections, of course, to the recovery of the passive by churches—or, to be more precise, to the recovery of churches by the passive. *One* is that we are lost in a semantic jungle. It makes no difference, this objection goes, whether a church's good works are done *through* it or *by* it so long as they are done. It makes no difference whether they are done to get a church *to* God or *from* God so long as they happen.

On the one hand the objection is valid. The main thing is the work, and if the work is not done, then there is little point in the church. On the other hand the objection is invalid. It makes a great deal of difference whether the work is done to get you to God or from God. It is the difference of power. It is the difference of size. More can be done with God than without. "I glorified thee on earth," Jesus said, "having accomplished the work which *thou* gavest me to do" (John 17:4). His work did not get him *to* God; it got him *from* God. And it was for that reason that it was powerful. It had the greatest *size* of any work in history.

*

Another objection to the recovery of the passive is that it is irrelevant. Again, the only thing that matters is what you do. Therefore the words you put on your actions are at best secondary and at worst irrelevant.

Agreed again. The words are not as important as the acts. And if you can get the acts without the words, then there is no point in wasting a person's time on Sunday morning.

Unfortunately, however, there is a serious question whether we *will* get the acts without the words. The way it is said is often the key to the way it is done. Indeed it is often *not* done *until* it is said. The problem with Jesus was that he said all the wrong things. He was talking about the passive, about letting God happen rather than making God happen. "The kingdom of God is preached" (Luke 16:16), he said. And he was executed for blasphemy, not for miracles, for what he said, not for what he did. The church today, as we all know, really *says* very little, therefore is rarely crucified, and therefore rarely demonstrates power.

*

A *third* objection to letting it happen through the church rather than by the church is that it is impractical. It won't work. If I ran my business that way, the objection goes, I'd be out on my ear tomorrow morning.

But would you? A man took his management team out of town, set up the conditions for the passive to operate at a local resort, took himself out of the picture, and in two days that team came up with fifty-six new product ideas.

Indeed, it could be argued that the reason the church is so anemic is that it has not acted passively. It has set up can-do goals. It has insisted on getting the credit. It has rarely risked anything other than what it is sure will "work."

*

A *fourth* objection to the recovery of the passive is that it is too easy. We no longer have anything to *do* as churches. This is what grates the most. To think that something could happen without our making it happen. To think that it could happen through us rather than by us. Tell an active person he no longer needs to be active, and he has visions of retirement at thirty. That gets to him.

This is the fundamental objection to the recovery of the passive. That it is not religion but escapism. *I* am no longer responsible—good, old middle-class rugged-individualist me. If it is going to be done through me rather than by me, then let whatever it is that is doing it through me, do it. It is no longer *my* ball game. God will do it. It's all part of God's plan. Predestination. Determinism. Fatalism. "Whatever will be will be." Defeatism. In a word: if it's all grace, then there's no need to work. If it's all grace, then there is no need for a church to act.

*

"By no means!" cried St. Paul (Rom. 6:2, 7:7, *et pas.*). It is what Peter was trying to get Jesus to do, and Jesus refused to do it. He called him "Satan" to his face. Not to act is a church member's greatest temptation, just as an active person's greatest temptation is not to be passive. "We are . . . created . . .," wrote the Ephesians churchmember, *"for* good works" (Eph. 2:10).

Two kinds of activity are possible for passive churches. One is optional, the other not. One does not work, the other does. One is to work your way to God; the other, from God. Take the first. Working our way to God does not work, but it does have value. Its value is to show us that it does not work. That *we* cannot do it. That we need more than ourselves to make it in the religious dimension, just as we need more than ourselves to make it in the business dimension and the community dimension and so on. "If it had not been for the law," Paul said, "I should not have known sin" (Rom. 7:7). If I had not *tried* to make it on my own as a good Pharisee, he was saying, I would *not* have discovered that *I* could not make it. And that is a very important thing for active churches to discover. It has immense value. They find they can do nothing when they have tried to do everything.

However, we do *not* have to make this discovery by *that* route. There are more ways than one to God. More accurately, there are more ways than one from God to us. People are different. That is why the first activity is optional. You do not *have* to work your way to God to find that you *cannot* work your way to God. For many church members, yes. For most church members, perhaps. But for all people, no.

Moses was minding his own business when God happened. So was Jeremiah, a teenager. So was Amos, a businessman. So was Saul, a young man. So were Peter, James, John. None of them was engaged in the struggle to find God. None of them was working his way to God. Their stories are characterized by nothing so much as routineness. They are plain, average, ordinary people doing plain, average, ordinary things when God happens. We cannot limit God to our penchant for activism. God *can* come that way, make no mistake. But God does not *have* to come that way. And when he doesn't many people get "fed up with the church" and leave.

It is all a matter of who you are. If your temperament is activist, then drive. Do everything you can to find God. Do all the right things. Read all the right books. Think all the right thoughts.

But there are other ways to God. If your temperament is passivist, then wait. It can happen that way too. It *did* happen that way to ordinary person after ordinary person in the Bible. No, not in the Bible. In history. They were people. They were human beings. They lived. They *were* chosen.

*

Either way, works are no longer optional. Once chosen, a church has no choice. It *has* to work. No, not justified by work. Certainly not justified by faith. But justified by grace. "When Israel was a child, I loved him, and out of Egypt I called my son" (Hos. 11:1). The works *show* the grace. They do not earn it. *Nothing* can earn it. "The Son can do *nothing*," Jesus said, "of his own accord" (John 5:19). "This is *not* your own doing" (Eph. 2:8). "I glorified thee on earth, having accomplished the work *thou* gavest me to do."

God acts; man reacts. Passive action is responsive action. It is reaction. The disciples had no idea what they were getting in for. It certainly wasn't the growth of an institution. But they reacted; they went. Paul had no idea what would happen to him, but he let it happen. He reacted; he went. He *did* what he felt he was being *told* to do.

Grace *means* work, or it is not grace. Grace means performance. The contract is drawn; the parties sign; you do your job. There is no such thing as a nominal church member. It is a contradiction in terms. You were hired to do a job. You were chosen to perform. If there are no works, then there was no grace. It is not optional. "What does the Lord *require* of you?" (Mic. 6:8). Not ask. Not suggest. Not encourage. Not implore. But require. And the answer is that churches are to do the *work* of justice and the *work* of love. If that means loss of members, fine.

The *point* of the grace *is* the work. It is your *job* as a church member to whom God has happened. You are a person through whom God *is* happening. "Let your light so shine before men," Jesus said, "that they may see your *good works.*" He did not say "see your faith." Nobody cares about your faith. We have it all backwards in the Protestant church, which is why the church is so fat when it should be so lean. It is not grace, faith, and works. It is grace, works, and faith. The faith comes *after.* It is what you are left with after the experience. It is what you have when the experience is gone, when the work is done. Precisely the problem with the church is that it has been long on faith and short on works. Everybody stands up on Sunday morning and confesses his faith, and then we go out and zap the guy at the office. We zap our own children. We zap the "Commies" and the "gooks" and the competition. It isn't the faith any more; it's the works. "He will render to every man according to his works," Paul said (Rom. 2:6). He did not say faith. He did not say ideas. He did not say belief. He said works. "If I have all *faith,* so as to remove mountains," he said, "but have not *love,* I am *nothing*" (1 Cor. 13:2). A church which is all faith and no works is nothing. It is *not* a church. Very few churches dare to risk anything that will *work.*

*

But who ever loves enough? Who ever is just enough? Who ever works *from* God enough? No one. *But that is not an excuse not to work.* It is not an excuse not to act. It is not an excuse for churches to give up and say "Whatever will be will be." Just because we cannot do everything does not mean we cannot do something. Indeed, Jesus was dumbfounded by what we *could* do, not on our own getting *to* God but with God's help getting *from* God. "Truly, truly, I say to you, he who believes in me will also do the works that *I* do; and *greater works than these will he do*" (John 14:12).

It was preposterous, but there it was. You will do *more* rather than less. "What more are you doing than others?" (Matt. 5:47). It is the point of the passive. It was the difference of power. It was the difference of size. We haven't begun to do what we're capable of doing as churches. It is the point of going passive. When it is done through us rather than by us, then we will at last do the big things. No, we will not love enough. No, we will not be just enough. Yes, we will lose members. But we will do more—more than we had ever done before, more than we ever dreamed would be possible.

> For this commandment which I command you this day is *not* too hard for you, neither is it far off. It is *not* in heaven, that you should say, "Who will go up for us to heaven, and bring it to us, that we may hear it and do it?" *Neither* is it beyond the sea, that you should say, "Who will go over the sea for us, and bring it to us, that we may hear it and do it?" But the word is very near you; it is in your mouth and in your heart, *so that you can do it* (Deut. 30:11–14).

Yes, it will be tough for churches, but so what? The passive assignments are always the toughest ones. The jobs we are given, the assignments we are told to do, the agenda we are shown, the minutes we write in our works. The church are the people who *do* those sorts of things. Anybody can be active; few can be passive. "Paul, a *slave* of Jesus Christ" (Rom: 1:1). It was the epitome of the passive. It *was* God. "Through love be slaves of one another" (Gal. 5:13). It *was* God. "He . . . emptied himself, taking the form of a slave" (Phil. 2:6, 7). It *was* God. God *is* what we find ourselves doing for justice. God *is* what we find ourselves doing for love. God *is* what we find ourselves doing as pared, lean, joyous groups of people called churches.

3

THE LOCAL CHURCH'S DAMASCUS

It is one thing to say let God happen. It is another thing to say how God happens. It is one thing to say let God happen though the church. It is another thing to say let God happen to the church. It is one thing to say work your way from God. It is another thing to explain how God works his way to you. Obviously the key to the passive is how God happens. How *does* a person become a church member, let alone remain one?

Equally obvious is that God can happen in any number of ways. "The wind blows where it wills" (John 3:8), Jesus said. But when we say that God can happen any way, we leave a lot up in the air. It is better to bring it down to earth and say here is one way God did happen. And what a way. If God had not happened this way, there is considerable doubt that the church would exist, either large or small.

When you analyze all the evidence, when you read all the letters, when you boil it all down, what do you find about how God happened to one of the first church members, Paul?

I

First, you find, among other things, that Paul gave it all he had. He was committed. His religion was the biggest thing in his life.

He did everything he could to make God happen through him and to him.

> I am a Jew, . . . brought up in this city at the feet of Gamaliel, educated according to the strict manner of the law of our fathers, being zealous for God (Acts 22:3).
>
> Are they Hebrews? So am I. Are they Israelites? So am I. Are they descendants of Abraham? So am I (2 Cor. 11:22).
>
> Brethren, I am a Pharisee, a son of Pharisees (Acts 23:6).

You couldn't get more religious than that.

Now as we have seen, this is *not* the way it has to be for everyone. A person doesn't have to give it all he has before he discovers that God is giving it all *he* has. "The wind blows where it wills." But this is the way it was for Paul. Thirty years old.[1] Member of the establishment. Well educated. Knew his religion by heart. Nationalist. Activist. Quite similar to many present-day American church members.

So often we expect miracles to happen when we have done nothing to make them happen. More accurately: when we have done nothing to recognize them when they happen. Oh, we say, I could never have a Damascus Road experience like Paul. But how can we say that when we are not even *on* the Damascus Road?

God comes because of what we do. No, not always. No, not even necessarily. "The wind blows where it wills." But this is the way God came for Paul. And he was young. He was aggressive. He had a college education. And he was giving it everything he had.

II

Second, he was on the wrong track. He was doing everything to find he could do nothing. No, it doesn't have to be that way. You can find you can do nothing by *not* doing everything, but Paul couldn't. We too, perhaps, have to do everything before we find we can do nothing. God happens. There are *no limits* on how he can happen, but he did happen for this young middle-class activist in this way. And it could be that this is the way he has to happen for other middle-class activists in statistically declining American churches.

Paul *had* to discover he was on the wrong track. No, it did not come easily. No, it did not come gradually. It came suddenly, and it came violently, but it had to come. This is the way it had to be for him. No, it is not the way it has to be for everyone, but it is the way it had to be for this young executive. He had to discover he was wrong.

He thought he was working from God. He was actually working to God. He thought he was letting God happen. He was actually making God happen. He thought God was working through him. "I am a Pharisee." God couldn't work through anybody any more than that. But the fact of the matter was that God had not yet happened to him; so God could not happen through him. In spite of all the Sunday school, all the church, all the religion of his fathers, all the education, all the middle-class hard work, *God had not yet happened.* The active church member had not yet become passive. And that probably holds true for two-thirds of every church in America.

Paul would not be passive—not on his own. It was too much to expect. It wasn't his style. It had to happen *to* him. He could not *make* it happen. This was one thing that Paul could not do. Yes, he had to try to do it. That was his style. That was the way it had to be for him to find God, to *be found* by God. But no, *he* could not do it. That was not *God's* style. *All* Paul could do was discover that *he* could not do it, and he could not even discover *that* on his own. He had to have help. God *was* the help. "And when the blood of Stephen thy witness was shed, *I* also was standing by and approving, and keeping the garments of those who killed him" (Acts 22:20).

Stephen showed Paul he was on the wrong track. It was sudden. It was violent. It was before his very eyes. Stephen had happened. Paul had done nothing to make him happen. Stephen came before Paul and the others to tell them they were on the wrong track. And they reacted the way any middle-class activist church member would. They became defensive. They killed him. "I also was standing by and approving."

The activist needs somebody, some one other human being, who, at great risk to himself or herself, will show the activist he is on the wrong track because the activist *cannot find that out on his own.* He is too mesmerized by his activity, his profit and loss statements, his politics, his church, his wars. Tragic as it may sound, America needed her young men to die for her in Vietnam to show her she was on the wrong track. Tragic as it may sound, Paul needed Stephen to die for him to show him he was on the wrong track. Paul needed someone, as we all do, to be *Jesus* to him. God was in *Stephen* reconciling *Paul* to himself.[2] That *was* God for Paul. God was coming at Paul. He was happening to him. The active "churchman" was becoming passive.

III

Then God happened. The Damascus Road was second; Stephen was first. He was minding his own business. He was doing his job. It was typically middle class. When he was flattened. "About noon a great light from heaven suddenly shone about me. And I fell to the ground and heard a voice saying to me, 'Saul, Saul, why do you persecute me?'" (Acts 22:6–7).

No, we will never know exactly how it happened, but that is hardly the point. We don't know exactly how it happened at the resurrection either, but that is not the point. The point is that, whatever was happening, it was happening *to* him, not *because* of him. It was being done *to* him not *by* him. God *was* what knocked him to the ground. God *was* what turned him around. God *was* what made the active man passive.

This is the point of religion. It is why people still go to church every week. It is why we can't stay away. It is why we are on the edge of our pews. God *is* what is coming at a person. He is the objective. For one hour we concentrate, not on what we can do, but on what can be done *to* us. And then on what can be done *through* us. They are where the power is. God *is* whatever objectifies me. That is the point of the transcendent. God *is* what transcends *my* ability to make it happen. "I am he who causes to happen what happens," he said to Moses (see Exod. 3:14). We have gone overboard on the subjective. God is more than Kierkegaard's "passionate inwardness." He is every person's passionate outwardness.

Paul had *nothing* to do with this experience. It happened to him. He did not cause it to happen. He didn't even *let* it happen. You can't even give an active church member *that*. The popular idea is to say, "Let go, let God." But Paul *didn't* let go. He held on tight—all the way up to when it happened.

> I persecuted the church of God violently and tried to destroy it (Gal. 1:13).

Then it happened.

> Saul, still breathing threats and murder against the disciples . . . went to the high priest and asked him for letters . . . so that if he found any belonging to the Way . . . he might bring them bound to Jerusalem (Acts 9:1–2).

Then it happened.

> I not only shut up many of the saints in prison, . . . but when they were put to death I cast my vote against them. And I punished them often in all the synagogues and tried to make

them blaspheme; and in raging fury against them, I persecuted them even to foreign cities (Acts 26:10–11).

I persecuted this Way to the death (Acts 22:4).

Then it happened.

So what are you saying—that we have to give all we have to
going it on the wrong track? Yes. And that is precisely what we
do in our churches. We are on the wrong track. We are out-
Pauling Paul. We are doing it completely right by doing it completely wrong.

We have persecuted Jesus. It's not only that churches have
killed people by not giving them enough food at Christmas and
Easter and throughout the rest of the year. It's not only that
churches have jailed people by starving the social action re-
sources in their communities to help keep people out of jails. And
it's not only that churches have persecuted Jesus around the
world by starving missionaries out of foreign countries because
of our steadfast refusal to tithe.

IV

It is that we do not recognize Jesus when he comes. Paul did
not recognize Jesus in Stephen. And Paul did not recognize Jesus
by the side of the road. He had to have help. Help had to come.
God had to come. God *is* coming at us all the time only we do not
recognize him. And we do not recognize him because we are too
busy doing it on our own. Whatever it is, we are too busy doing
it on our middle-class, educated, activist, church-member own.

The word *revelation* meant God coming out of concealment.[3] It
was the point of religion. God was doing it all the time, only we
did not see. "*God* was pleased to reveal his Son to me" (Gal.
1:16), Paul exclaimed. But he didn't know it until someone had
helped him. Stephen helped. Stephen *was* Jesus. He gave himself

for Paul. That was the start, but not even that was enough. There had to be someone else to interpret for Paul what happened to him by the side of the road. Even though he had been flattened, he was still so much of an activist, still so *human,* that he had to have help in learning what had happened to him, in learning that he had to become passive. God *was* what helped him. God *was* what came to him in the form of a man who "came to me, and standing by me said to me, 'Brother Saul, receive your sight. . . . You will be a witness' " (Acts 22:13, 15).

"*Brother* Saul!" It was said by one of the people he was going to *kill.* The man was afraid. He didn't want to go, but God had happened to *him,* and he knew he must. "Go, for he [Paul] is a chosen instrument of mine" (Acts 9:15). And Ananias went.

God has come to you as a church member. Somewhere. Some time. It was a beginning. Somebody showed you, at great risk to himself or herself, that you were on the wrong track, that you were active when you should have been passive, that you were trying to make it happen when it *was* happening, that you were so intent on getting things done by you that you were preventing their being done to you and so they could never be done through you.

Your Ananias has come or is coming to you. You did nothing to deserve him. He is there to interpret what has happened to you. He is the gift of God. He *is* grace. You may never have known him or her before, but he is there. He is objective. He came to you; you did not come to him. God *is* the person who, at great risk to himself or herself, shows you that you are on the wrong track. And God *is* the person who, at great risk again, shows you how you are now on the right track only you did not know it.

Who are such people? They are everywhere. God is continually sending them. A girl stood up and said to a church how she had been outside and wanted to be inside. How the warm and beautiful people, symbolized in another girl standing beside her, had somehow, in spite of themselves, done the right thing in the wrong way, and been Stephen to her, and Ananias, and how now she wanted to be a chosen instrument with them. And then a boy got up and said how he had given it all he had and been on the wrong track and now on his road to his school and his family and his job it had come to him that maybe something could be done through him rather than by him because the warm and beautiful people had happened to him, too, and been Stephen to him, and Ananias.

The *church* are the people who, at great risk to themselves, show you you are on the wrong track by giving themselves for you, in whatever way, however small. The more your activity, the larger their gift. And the church are the warm and beautiful people who, when something has happened to you, however large, however small, come to you and say "Brother, receive your sight. This is the way it was for you. It was *God* happening to you. And now he will happen through you. You who once were active have now become passive. 'The old has passed away. Behold the new has come.' "[4]

NOTES

1. N. H. P. Hatch in *The Interpreter's Bible* (New York: Abingdon, 1951), vol. 7, p. 192.
2. 2 Cor. 5:19.
3. A. Oepke in G. Kittel, *Theological Dictionary of the New Testament* (Grand Rapids, Mich.: Eerdmans, 1965), vol. 3, p. 580.
4. 2 Cor. 5:17.

4

THE POINT IS TO BE OBJECTIFIED

You can wander into a church anywhere in America on Sunday morning, and the chances are there will be people there. Maybe not many people. Certainly fewer people than ten years ago. But still people. Something is happening that is worth coming to.

You can wander out of a church anywhere in America on a Sunday morning and vow never to go back. But something will linger. Something will haunt you. Something won't let you go.

It is that something which is the power of religion, and we belong to churches because of it. You don't go to church because you want to. You go because you have to, because you can't stay away. You're caught. You're hooked. You're out of control. It is the power of the objective. And, although it is there for everyone, not everyone has experienced it. Which is why church growth is not the point; being objectified is.

I

Now at first glance it may appear that religion is the power of the subjective. It is what *I* want. It is what works for me by explaining me to myself. But that is not the point of religion at all. Or if at all, only secondarily. The point of religion is God, not us.

Religion is objectivity. It is what exists apart from us. We have nothing to do with it. We don't "get religion." Religion gets us. And it does not depend on us for its existence. The little church at the corner of State and Main is going to be there long after us. It was there long before. It is a mute symbol of the power of the objective.

Yes, religion is subjectivity. It *is* passionate inwardness. It is love. But there is more to it than that. The real *power* of religion is its objectivity. Not what you do to it, but what it does to you. You don't go to church to lead a better life. You don't go to get peace of mind. You don't go to be happy. You go to be jolted out of yourself. You're not important. The only thing that matters on Sunday morning is what the objective, as one form of the passive, is going to do through you. "He who would lose his life will find it."

This is why there is no reason to be too upset by the "one-hour-a-week Christian." *If* the service has been a jolt, such a person should have had as large a dose of the objective as he can take for one week. The trouble, of course, is that most services aren't jolts and the objective doesn't get through.

It did for Isaiah. It is an example of how all worship should go. He found himself pounded by the objective. It got through all the forms which were trying to mediate it, which is precisely what the forms were meant to do. Even the choir itself, which is sometimes called the war department of the church, was transformed. He got through their singing to this: "Holy, holy, holy is the Lord of hosts" (Isa. 6:3).

Holy was the word which caught the objective. It came from the root for "separate," "set apart," "make distinct," "put at a distance from."[1] God is what we aren't. He is holy *before* he is loving. Indeed, "God *is* love" (1 John 4:8) is a very late sentiment in the Bible, not coming until the second century A.D.,[2] and it is a sentiment voiced as such only once. Why? Because the biblical writers were insistent that *the objective comes first. That* was where the power was. It is not what you do to God that counts, but what

God does to you. Only God can overcome the distance between himself and us. God *is* the distance. That's first. And God *is* what overcomes the distance. That's second.

The trouble begins when church members, as we invariably do, put second things first, when we try to subjectivize the objective. We are tough. We are bright. We have upper-middle-class incomes. And we can't stand distance. No one is going to tell us we can't come near. No one is going to tell us to stay back. And yet that is precisely what the objective says. Stay back. No one shall touch my holy mountain (Exod. 19:12). Do not come near or you will die.

The objective is unapproachable. You do not approach it; it approaches you. How do you get to the mountain? You never get to the mountain. The mountain gets to you. Ah, but a church member *goes* to church. That isn't you. You'd a lot rather be home with the Sunday paper. You didn't go. You were *brought.* Remember, you're hooked by the objective.

It is the remoteness of our religion that we are in danger of losing. We do very well on the near side of things. We have small groups. We get very close. But we are in trouble on the far side. Like the moth to the flame, we cannot keep our distance. And that is what desacralizes our churches. We cannot stand the objective; so we do everything from build "our" buildings to muzzle our clergy to finally, in disenchantment, leave.

It goes back into the human condition. The king in the early days of Isaiah was Uzziah. King Uzziah could not keep his distance. He came into the temple to burn his own incense, to use a form which had been reserved for distance. It was not his to use. But he was tough. He was bright. The nation had never been in better shape. Just as he could bridge his way to success, so he could bridge his way to God. He failed, and his punishment, according to the ancient story, was the epitome of distance. He became a leper, was exiled to a leper's house, and was told ever after to keep his distance.

The point, then, of worship is not only to mediate closeness but distance. "Holy, holy, holy." It was the objective pounding him. The point of reading the Bible is to find out how distance overcomes *itself* and is transmuted into closeness. And the point of prayer is not to find out who *I* am. That is subjective and secondary. The point of prayer is to find out who *God* is. It is to *be* found *by* God. That is objective and first.

II

All right. So we have the objective coming at us through churches—and, of course, elsewhere.[3] We have it mediated by the three big objectifiers—worship, Bible, prayer. *What* is mediated? What does the objective *do?* What are the evidences of its *power?*

First, in bald terms, it tells church members how bad they are. And for something to do that, it would have to be powerful indeed, because we are normally not reminded of the far side of our human nature. Not if we're middle class and making it "on our own." Not if we're upper class as Isaiah was and only eighteen.[4] And certainly not if we are in "successful" American churches.

Nevertheless, that is what happened. Isaiah's experience was so intense that form vanished into substance, subjectivity into objectivity, and objectivity into perspective.

> Woe is me! For I am lost; for I am a man of unclean lips, and I dwell in the midst of a people of unclean lips (Isa. 6:5).

But how did he *know* that? He knew it because he had been shown it.

> Woe is me! For I am lost; . . . *for* my eyes have seen the King, the Lord of hosts! (Isa. 6:5.)

When he experienced distance, *then* he experienced lostness, the epitome of distance. When he experienced God, *then* he experienced Isaiah. When the objective found him, *then* he found himself. First the objective, *then* the subjective.

Sure. Fine. But who ever is going to have that intense an experience in worship? What about all those other people who were worshiping with Isaiah? Obviously it didn't affect them that way. That's why he was a prophet and they weren't. That's why he is a prophet and we aren't.

Not at all. Forget them. The objective is coming at *you,* church member, all the time. Grace is serendipity. You go to church. That's the power of the objective. No, maybe not an Isaiah experience, but you *are* there. You *are* reading the Bible. It obviously isn't you. You *do* pray. It obviously isn't you. You'd rather talk or go to sleep or forget it. It *has* to be the objective because it *can't* be you.

And what about all the other experiences of a church member's life in which the objective was coming at us? We were born. We had nothing to do with it. We were educated. We had nothing to do with it. It was all a matter of where we lived, and that was a matter of our parents' income. We were married. We didn't marry someone. He or she married us. What did we do to deserve it? We were *given* a job. We didn't earn it. We were *given* intellectual equipment. Intelligence, according to the latest scientific data, is 75 percent heredity.[5] And, to take it one step further, "substantially higher average I.Q.'s are consistently found among members of the higher social strata."[6] The myth of the self-made man is just that, a myth. But it persists because the subjective persists in trying to overcome the objective. It is King Uzziah all over again, and that may be fine if that's our style. But it has nothing to do with the *point* of church, nothing to do with a jolt, nothing to do with discovering the far side of our human nature because we have *been* discovered *by* the objective *through* our churches.

"Woe is me! For I am lost." It was the ultimate in distance. It came *after* the objective. It could not have come before. There was no need. There was no standard. Against all subjective standards, churches do very well indeed. "We're doing the best we can," we say. "We do as well as the next church." "We pay the mortgage." And we list all the other brilliants which excuse us from having to measure up to an *objective* standard by which we know we will *fail.*

This is where Paul was so helpful. As any great religious leader, he recovered the objective. The objective recovered *him.* It showed him that, no matter how hard he tried, he could not overcome the distance, he could not subjectivize the objective, he could not move the mountain; it had to move itself. "Since all have sinned and fall *short* of the glory of God, they are justified by his *grace* as a gift" (Rom. 3:23).

*

Second, we are forgiven. It is a great power, an enormous power. It is the objective. "Behold, . . . your guilt is taken away, and your sin forgiven" (Isa. 6:7). When Isaiah experienced that, the power coursed through him. Nothing is more powerful in a person's life than forgiveness. "Take heart, my son; your sins are forgiven. . . . Rise, take up your bed and go home" (Matt. 9:2, 6).

You can't forgive yourself. You have to *be* forgiven. Another person has to do it. The objective has to do it. Forgiveness is the most important thing ever mediated by the three objectifiers— worship, Bible, prayer, which are themselves mediated by the church when it is the church. Why? Because when you are forgiven, everything opens up. You feel you can do anything. *The mountain has moved to you.*

Sure. Fine. But isn't this forgiveness for the few? It's what everyone wants but only a few get. We join a church wanting the power. Then we do not experience the power, and we give it all up. How many Isaiahs are there? How many Isaiahs can there be?

Go at it this way. Go back to the roots, back to first things first, back to the objective. You don't feel forgiven because you don't feel bad because you don't feel the holy. And you don't feel the holy because you don't feel jolted by one of the three objectifiers. And you don't feel jolted by one of the three objectifiers because they haven't pounded at you hard enough. And they haven't pounded at you hard enough because very few churches really *dare* to pound *and* because you wouldn't *let* yourself *be* pounded. *You* had to do all the pounding. *You* had to overcome the distance. Step back. You're getting too close to the mountain. You can't forgive yourself. You have to be forgiven. The mountain has to come to you.

Distance. Allow yourself to feel fear. That is what Jesus meant by becoming children—to feel our feelings. "The silence of these infinite spaces frightens me," said Pascal. He felt the dread of distance. We are a long way from home. We have "miles to go before we sleep." Time is running out. We have much to do, and we have not done it. Feel that distance from yourself and be afraid. It may be the way that God is coming at you. Or feel your distance from ultimate meaning and be afraid. It may be the way that God is coming at you.

Above all, do *not* subjectivize the objectifiers. Let them do their work on you. Yes, they will do their work anyway. They are that powerful. But if you refuse, with Isaiah, to impede them, and beat down your King Uzziah, who knows, you too, at an early age, may experience the power of forgiveness.

*

Finally, over the catalyst of forgiveness, the church member goes. That is how powerful the objective is. It is not enough to sit around and look profound and experience our goodness. Our goodness, or better yet our forgiven-ness, is always proved by what we do. "And I heard the voice of the Lord saying, 'Whom shall I send, and who will go for us?' Then I said, 'Here I am! Send me.' And he said, 'Go . . .'" (Isa. 6:8–9).

Isaiah was nothing; but he was everything. He was worthless; but he had value. He was lost, the epitome of distance; but now he was found, the epitome of distance overcome by distance. The objective had been at work. Now he would do what he *had* to do.

No, it wasn't he. The objective was too powerful for that. It was the objective using him. "Whom shall *I* send?" It wasn't his thing. Who wants to go out and tell people how bad they are? Who wants to be used to bring the fear, the dread, the terror of distance that way?

Ah, but he went. That is what made him a prophet. We may know our badness and even feel forgiveness, but we won't go. That's why we're just folks while he was Isaiah. It's why we're groups of people when we could be churches.

Yes, that's one way to argue it. But another way is that if the objective has done its work we *will* go. We *will* do what we *have* to do. We can't *not* go. The objective is *that* powerful.

The Bible, perhaps the greatest objectifier of all time, is nothing more nor less than a book about plain, average, ordinary people like us who, as it was once said, were snatched from the banality of their lives. Who was Isaiah? Well born. Well educated. Well married. With a good job. Young. Smart. Tough. Rich. Religious. A typical American "church member."

It can happen again. That is the point of the Bible. It is the point of prayer. It is the point of worship. It is the power of the objective. God *is* what condemns us. God *is* what forgives us. God *is* what sends us.

Holy, holy, holy is the Lord of hosts.

The church is in business to recover the holy, to *be* recovered *by* it, to be objectified. That is the point of the church. If it grows, fine. If it doesn't grow, equally fine. The point is not growth but objectification, not size but jolt.

NOTES

1. J. Muilenburg in *The Interpreter's Dictionary of the Bible* (New York: Abingdon, 1962), vol. 2, p. 617; G. A. Smith, *The Book of Isaiah* (London: Harper, 1927), vol. 1, p. 63.
2. A. N. Wilder in *The Interpreter's Bible* (New York: Abingdon, 1957), vol. 12, p. 215.
3. It has always been a mistake—often tragic and always pointless—to limit the activity of God to the church. *Extra ecclesiam nulla salus* (outside the church there is no salvation) is as senseless today as when it was first decreed.
4. C. R. North in Muilenburg, *op. cit.*, vol. 2, p. 732.
5. B. Berelson and G. Steiner, *Human Behavior: An Inventory of Scientific Findings* (New York: Harcourt, 1964), p. 217.
6. *Ibid.*, p. 222.

5

THE POINT IS TO BE MADE REAL

Religion is not only objectivity, it is realism. It is what really counts. It is what really happens. It is more real than anything that has ever happened to a church member. There is no greater reality. This is it. The passive has tightened its grip. If there is no grip, then there is no church.

I

It begins in confrontation. Church members are confronted by a reality that is greater than they, and there is nothing they can do about it. They are confronted, and they *know* it is the biggest thing in their lives.

Jeremiah was a teenager (Jer. 1:6). He lived in a suburb (Jer. 1:1). He was from a good family.[1] He was warm-hearted. Gentle. Well trained in the religion of his people.[2] Then it happened. Reality struck. It was the realest thing that had ever happened to him. It was really Jeremiah, and it was something so much bigger than Jeremiah that he knew he was in touch with reality itself.

Now the word of the Lord came to me saying,

> "Before I formed you in the womb I knew you,
> and before you were born I consecrated you;
> I appointed you a prophet to the nations."
>
> (Jer. 1:4–5)

No, he didn't will it. It had *nothing* to do with him. *He* wasn't responsible. Reality hit him. He didn't hit reality. It was the antithesis of morality. He didn't choose. He *was* chosen. He had *nothing* to do with it. Yes, you make choices in this life. But yes, you *are* chosen. The realest things are not the things you choose but the things that choose you. As we have seen, we were born. We were educated. We were loved. We were promoted. We were given our religion. We were given our uniqueness. We were given ourselves. Reality is in the passive.

Jeremiah didn't even *let* it happen. It happened. That was how powerful the reality of it was. There was nothing *he* could do to bring it. There was nothing *he* could do to prevent it. It happened regardless of him. Regardless of how he thought. Regardless of how he felt. Regardless of what he did. There was no way he could shake it. The passive had tightened its grip. He knew it was real because he could not shake what was happening. He knew it was real because he couldn't *not* be confronted and still *be* Jeremiah.

That is how a church member knows it is real. When you can't shake it. When it shakes you. When it won't let you go. When it is there morning, noon, and night. When you can't eat. When you can't sleep. When there is no place to run. No place to hide. No place to cower. No place to hit your head. Then you know you are being confronted. Then you know you are in the grip of something more powerful than you. Then you know you can't be yourself and escape the confrontation.

Jeremiah fought it. He fought it with everything he had, and he was only a teenager. "Ah, Lord God! Behold, I do not know how to speak, for I am only a youth" (Jer. 1:6). That's how he knew

it was reality. Because he fought so hard. That's how he knew it
was a confrontation that would change his life. Because he knew
he couldn't do it. He knew he couldn't face it. He knew he
couldn't bear it. If he could *stand* it, then it wasn't a confrontation. It was a meeting. A coffee break.

You can't help yourself. That's how you know it is real. If you
can help yourself, then it isn't the passive. It's still the active.
It's still you calling all the plays. And that is precisely what it can
not be, not if you're going to be in the grip of the passive,
not if you're going to be jolted by the objective, not if you're
going to be in touch with reality, not if you're going to be a
church.

It happened to all of them. Moses, tortured by the reality of
what was happening to him, fighting it all the way (Exod. 3). And
losing. Knowing he would lose. Knowing he couldn't win. Knowing it was hopeless. He couldn't help himself. Isaiah, tortured by
the guilt of his confrontation, knowing it was too big for him,
knowing it was the biggest thing in his life, knowing he would
have to do whatever he was told to do because it was that real (Isa.
6). It *was* reality. Jesus, thrown into the wilderness for forty days
and forty nights, wrestling, as Jacob at the River Jabbok (Gen.
32), with the temptation to escape reality, to seize the initiative,
to be active rather than passive, subjective rather than objective,
idealistic rather than realistic (Matt. 4). And then Jesus at the end,
and this is the horror of it, now knowing where the reality had
gone. "My God, my God, why hast thou forsaken me?" (Matt.
27:46).

II

So what began as confrontation continues as destruction. A
church member's ability to fight is destroyed. That is what *makes*
him a church member. Our ability to resist is destroyed. Our
ability to raise up our inadequacies as our only defense is

destroyed. *We* are destroyed because reality always fights back. Remember, it is reality.

> Do not say, "I am only a youth";
> for to all to whom I send you you shall go,
> and whatever I command you you shall speak.
> (Jer. 1:7)

Reality beats down our objections. It is not in the interest of reality to lose. Of course he was young. Of course he was inexperienced. Of course he had no ability to speak. That was the proof that it was reality and not he. *He* couldn't do it. Therefore it *had* to be reality.

You know it is real because you know it can't be you. You feel yourself slipping. You feel the fight being drained. You feel that while all your excuses are subjectively valid they have no standing before the jolt of the objective. No standing before the onslaught of the real. You feel that although where you are may be real, where you ought to be is realer.

Reality destroys what it creates that it may create it better. "To destroy and to overthrow, to build and to plant" (Jer. 1:10). The temple will be destroyed. The people will be destroyed. Jeremiah will be destroyed. This is suffering: to destroy what you have built in order to build it better. Reality suffers with us.

But it has to be if reality is to have its way. If it isn't going to have its way, then it isn't reality. It isn't powerful enough, not yet. The confrontation has not yet come, much less the destruction.

What Jeremiah had to realize was that *he* made no difference. And that is hard for church members to realize, that is, see the reality of. It made no difference to reality that he was inadequate. It would have made no difference if he had felt he *was* adequate. Nobody is adequate to do the work of reality. If we were, it would be us and not reality. But that is the one thing reality cannot accept. It has to be done through us not by us. Reality has to be adequate for us. We can never be adequate for reality.

In a word, then, Jeremiah's ego was submerged. It was buried. More accurately, it was destroyed. And again, it is the thread that goes all the way back. Every one of the realists had his ego destroyed. Moses, destroyed. Isaiah, destroyed. Samuel, destroyed. James, destroyed. Paul, destroyed. "It is no longer *I* who live, but *Christ* who lives in me" (Gal. 2:20). It is *the* reality for church members.

Now it could be argued, as it always is, that these were exceptional people. And they were. But only on the *other* side of their confrontation. On this side they were much like us. One was a shepherd. One, a priest. One, a youth. One, a carpenter. One, a member of the establishment.

The key is to get to the other side. Of course we would all like to say, "It is no longer I who live." Of course we would all like our egos destroyed that a better ego might be built. How does it happen?

It *is* happening. It is happening *all* the time. Reality is that powerful. It is constantly coming at us. Look at what you fight. Look at what you can't shake. Look at what shows you your inadequacies and then comes back and makes light of them. What is it in your life that keeps coming back and back and back? That *is* reality. That *is* your religion. The others who can't shake it either *are* the church.

III

But it is never enough to leave it at that. It is one thing to be confronted. Another to be destroyed. But there is always something more. And the something more is that the church is given something to do. The Phoenix rises from the ashes of its own destruction. The resurrection comes.

> Then the Lord put forth his hand and touched my mouth; and the Lord said to me,

"Behold, I have put my words in your mouth.
  See, I have set you this day over nations and over
      kingdoms,
  to pluck up and to break down,
  to destroy and to overthrow,
  to build and to plant."

(Jer. 1:9–10)

No, he could not do it. That was obvious. He was a teenager, and he was being asked to be a statesman. It was up to him to speak against the politics of the day and for the theology of yesterday. He couldn't do it, but that was the *point.* It was going to be done through him not by him. He was in the grip of the passive. It was that *real.*

Whoever said that a church could ever do anything for justice? Whoever said we had the time? Whoever said we had the ability? Whoever said we had the enthusiasm? Of course we can't. Of course we won't. Not on our own. But reality is coming at us, and we are *not* on our own. "I have put *my* words in *your* mouth." "Whatever *I* command you you shall speak." "*I* appointed *you.*" It's my job, not yours. I'm *using* you to do *my* job. You are my mouthpiece. Of course you don't know what to say. Of course you don't know what to do. That's the point. I say it through you. I do it through you. It's my job. I'm telling you to do my job. "I appointed you." You are my church.

He couldn't not do it. That is how powerful it was. He couldn't not do it and still *be* Jeremiah. He couldn't not do it and be *real.* He had to go. He had to speak. He had to destroy and to overthrow. He had to build and to plant. Not to have done so would have meant to deny reality, to be unreal. "The mass of men lead lives of quiet desperation," Thoreau said. We are unreal. We deny the real you, the real us, the real me. We don't do what really matters. We don't do what really counts. And the sands are running out.

Why don't we do it? Because we're scared. The confrontation

itself was terrifying enough. But then to be destroyed. And now to be sent. Jeremiah was afraid.

> Be not afraid . . . [reality had to say to him]
>   for I am with you to deliver you.
>
>   (Jer. 1:8)

"I am with you." That was all that mattered. It was that real, that powerful. "I will be with you," God said to Moses (Exod. 3:12). "I am with you always," Jesus said to his disciples (Matt. 28:20).

There was bound to be danger. There was bound to be hardship. There was bound to be suffering—incredibly deep, unbearable suffering. To the *church*. If there is no suffering, then there is no church. Its symbol is the *cross*.

Jeremiah couldn't have done it if reality had not been so powerful as to break through his fear. It was that real. It was that powerful. "I am with you to deliver you." He would have to be rescued. It was going to be that bad. There was no mitigating what he was getting into. There would be a thousand savage and lonely streets. There would be the heart of darkness. But he must not despair. He was doing what he had to do, and it would be all right. "I am with you to deliver you." Everything would be all right. It would be all right.

But not even that was enough. He had to have more. Here he was twenty-three years later looking back on what he had done,[3] and he realized that he had had to have more. When you are going into that much suffering, you have to have more. It was the only way Jeremiah could handle it. It had to be he, yes, but it had to be more. It had to be his destiny. It had to be in the stars. *They* had to have brought him here. *They* had to have brought him to this hour. In biblical language, he had to feel predestined. It was the same feeling Paul had to have. Without it they could not have done it. Without it they could not have gone on.

> Before I formed you in the womb I knew you,
> And before you were born I consecrated you.

You, God, have brought us to this hour. You, God, have confronted us. You, God, have destroyed us. You, God, have ordered us to go, to *be* the church.

NOTES

1. S. R. Hopper in *The Interpreter's Bible* (New York: Abingdon, 1956), vol. 5, p. 801.
2. *Ibid.,* p. 802.
3. *Ibid.,* p. 800.

6

THE POINT IS REVELATION

The problem for church members is really not what you might think it is. It is not, How can I lead a better life? It is not, How can I lead a fuller life? It is not, How can I lead a more meaningful life? It is the passive problem, How can meaning find *me*? How can I *be* filled? How can I be *made* better? In a word, the point is not, How can I find God, but How can God find me?

Now it might appear that these questions are actually the same, but they aren't. Far from it. The one depends on us; the other, on God. The one is a matter of our self-fulfillment; the other, a matter of God's self-fulfillment.

The difference is more than semantic. It turns the entire question around. And that is something that may be difficult if not impossible for middle- and upper-middle-class American church members. Religion is not a matter of how we get God. It is a matter of how God gets us. It has everything to do with God; nothing to do with us. God is what matters; not us. God is what counts; not us. This is the one enterprise which we don't run. That makes some upset by membership loss, others nonchalant. "I did it," God said through Ezekiel, "that they might know that I am the Lord" (see Ezek. 39:7).

All right. *How* do you know it?

I

One, something is happening whether we know it or not. Remember, it has everything to do with God and nothing to do with us. It may affect us, but we don't affect it, not in the slightest. It may be effected through us, but we don't effect it. Not at all. It is the cause; we are the effect. God acts; we react. God is everything; we are nothing. God makes himself known to us; we do not make ourselves know to God.

OK. But that's a pretty blunt position. It is all God and no us. That makes us puppets. Precisely. That is the point—*to* make us puppets, to reduce us to *exactly* the place where everything is done *through* us *by* God, where he pulls *all* the strings. *Then* we have become a church.

God reveals himself; we do not reveal God. God discloses himself; we do not disclose God. God lifts the veil from himself; we do not lift the veil from God. More accurately from the Hebrew tradition: God speaks—we listen. And it is happening all the time whether we know it or not.

To what purpose? Not love. Not "ethics." Not truth. Not beauty. Not goodness. Not education. Not positive thinking. Not self-fulfillment. God reveals himself for one reason only—to reveal himself. "I did it that they might know that I am the Lord." That was *all* that mattered. *Everything* else was secondary. *Everything* else followed.

"I am who I am" (Exod. 3:14) is the most important statement in the Bible. It was when God revealed himself to Moses. It is more important than the Red Sea. It is more important than Mount Sinai. It is more important than the Promised Land. It is more important than Ezekiel. It is more important than Jesus. It was God's first great act of self-revelation. Yes, he had revealed himself to Abraham, Isaac, and Jacob. Yes, he had established the covenant and given them the Promised Land. But this was the first time he had revealed his name. "By my name the Lord I did not make myself known to them" (Exod. 6:2). And it was out of this revelation that he said: "I will take you for my people, and I will be your God" (Exod. 6:7).

God's revelation of himself is *all* that matters. *Everything* follows from it. It is the central problem of church membership. *Everything* is secondary to it. Of course I will do God's will if I only *know* what it is. Of course I will obey if I only *hear* the commands. Of course I will create the beautiful, do the good, know the truth if I am only *told* what the beautiful is, *told* what the good is, *told* what the truth is. God's self-revelation is everything, and it is going on all the time. "Lo, I am with you always, to the close of the age" (Matt. 28:20). "I did it that they might know that I am the Lord." And he says it through Ezekiel again and again, more than any other book in the Bible. "I did it that they might know that I am the Lord."

Fine. But *how* do you know?

II

Two, you get out of the abstract into the concrete. You come out of the stratosphere into the atmosphere. You get down to specifics. You get down to people. You get down to one person. You get down, in this case, to Ezekiel.

That's what the Bible is. It is a book of case studies of people who *knew.* They knew that God was revealing himself to them. They knew what God's will was. They knew what the good, the true, the beautiful were. They knew what they were being told to do, and they knew that they would do it.

That's why we teach the Bible in churches. We teach the case-study method just the way Harvard Business School teaches the case-study method. Only we do not teach it enough. "Liberal" churches are notorious for being brilliant on the secondary and ignorant on the primary. They emphasize "social justice" and deemphasize reading the Bible. But what sense does that make when we could emphasize justice more if we would only *read* the Bible? Instead, the only people who read the Bible are our children in our church schools. We forget that Jesus blessed the children and taught the adults.

Ezekiel—son of Buzi, family of Zadok, priest, thirty years old,[1] suburb of Babylon, Tel-abib. On the banks of the Chebar, July 21, 592 B.C.,[2] the Lord breaks his silence. "Son of man, stand upon your feet, and I will speak with you" (Ezek. 2:1).

First, God broke the silence, not Ezekiel. Remember, God is revealing himself. We do not reveal God.

Second, beyond that there are no conditions. It can happen any number of ways. There are many case studies. "The wind blows where it wills" (John 3:8), as we have seen. You can't limit the spirit. You can't limit the self-revelation of God.

Third, Ezekiel was young. This is not to say God will not reveal himself to you if you are old. It is only to say that Ezekiel was thirty. Jesus was the same. Jeremiah was a teenager. And that should give us old folks pause whenever we mock what we may call the religious excesses of the young—the Jesus people, the Dallas Explo, the young Jew, Bob Dylan.

Fourth, Ezekiel had it made. He lived in a suburban ghetto where the only foreigners were the police. They were all his own kind. There were all middle and upper class. They all belonged to the establishment. There was no low-income housing. Down the street was the president of the bank. Across was the senior partner in the leading law firm. Around the corner was a Teamsters vice-president.

Fifth, it happened long after he got his religion. Ezekiel had lived five years in the suburb. Before that he had lived all his life in the big city where he had learned his trade as a Zadokite priest. In other words, he had his religion long before his religion had him. A typical "church member."

Sixth, in spite of all that looked good on the surface, there was a lot going on under the surface in Ezekiel that was anything but good. He was being churned up all the time. Now again, this is not a condition of God's self-disclosure. And if it doesn't fit you, fine. But it did fit Ezekiel. It did fit this young suburban priest. And it may be that because it *was* a condition for him it *should* be a condition for us and perhaps even *is* a condition for us.

Ezekiel was in exile. He was a long way from home. Yes, it was an easy exile. They could do what they wanted. They could worship as they pleased. They could even engage in business. But the fact of the matter was they were far from home. Their fate was up to the caprice of their captors. They had it hanging over them all the time. And, although it looked good on the middle-class surface, it was desperate underneath.

It was equally desperate back home; so Ezekiel had that churning him too. Remember, he was a member of the establishment; so when the votes weren't going the way he wanted them to in the city council, he grew anxious. On top of the bad voting was the national power struggle. It was time for an election—or selection. One man was king whom Ezekiel didn't like. Another man wanted to be king whom Ezekiel liked very much. And a third man, who carried a lot of weight, had just refused to support either of them.

The religion was also in a mess. Because the nation had lost, the God was gone. That's the way the popular mind read it.[3] Therefore the door had been opened to every conceivable attempt to water down the demands of the religion. There were no standards of church membership. You could come and go as you pleased. You could do what you liked. Nothing about sacrifice. Nothing about justice. Nothing about the self-revelation of God. "They are a rebellious house" (Ezek. 2:5).

III

So where does all this leave us? It leaves us with a young professional, member of the upper-middle-class estalishment, serene on the surface, a cauldron beneath.

Ah, but that was Ezekiel. He was a genius; we're not.

Precisely wrong. There is nothing in Ezekiel's background that suggests he was a genius. There is nothing that suggests he was the one to hear God speak. There is nothing to suggest that he more than anyone else should be the one to whom God would reveal himself.

The elitist argument is the weakest argument in religion. It may be a strong agrument when you're running a business, but it's a lousy argument when you're running a church. You can't program the spirit. You can't put it into a Univac computer. Nor can you take it down to the weather station and predict it. "The wind blows where it wills."

The fact of the matter was that God chose this individual. And this individual, as the case study shows, was a plain, average, ordinary Jaycee, serene on the surface and boiling beneath.

*

But only Ezekiel was chosen. Only *one* plain, average, ordinary citizen.

Not so. Jeremiah was doing in Jerusalem what Ezekiel was doing in Tel-abib. And they were doing it at the same time. Yes, that's only two out of a nation, but consider. On the one hand what they said was firmly believed by thousands. No, not by enough thousands to get elected. We all know prophets don't get elected. But by enough to realize that the word of God was not limited to these two men. The "faithful remnant" never forgot it, and churches exist today because they didn't.

On the other hand, so what if only two people were saying what needed to be said? Maybe that's what leadership is. "History is the lengthened shadow of a man," Emerson wrote. We need more upper-middle-class men and women hearing what needs to be heard so they will say what needs to be said. No, not many men and women. Just a few, who will *do* it. *That's* what we want in churches. And if that means membership loss, fine.

*

But nobody gets chosen any more. The Bible is written. The book is closed. The case studies have all been done.

Not so. The case studies are not only in the Bible. They're in us. That's the *point* of the biblical faith, that *we* are chosen—plain, average, ordinary church-member *us*. "I chose you," Jesus said to the disciples (John 15:16), twelve ordinary people. "Once you were no people," Peter said to a group of plain, average, ordinary people, "but now you are God's people" (1 Pet. 2:10). They were the *church*.

The revelation goes on. The thing that happened to Ezekiel is happening all the time. It is so powerful it does not stop. It cannot stop. It will not stop. It is God's "glory," his *kavoth*, his what-he-does-to-us-that-we-can't-do-to-him. "I did it that they might know that I am the Lord." "God making his appeal through us" (2 Cor. 5:20).

*

But look at Ezekiel's cauldron. That seems to be what did it. It worked on him. But I'm not in exile. Nothing is hassling me. My politics are OK. And my religion I can take or leave.

Fine. It doesn't have to be for you the way it was for Ezekiel. But watch it. The way it was for him worked. It released the power. He was "overpowered" (Ezek. 3:15). The word is his. If we are seriously interested in the religious problem, if we really want to be found by God, if we want to make the church experience work, it behooves us to look hard at this case, this man, this puppet.

You too may have your cauldron. You too may be upset with the direction of your country. You too may be upset with the direction of your church. You too may be in exile—far from home, far from the person you were meant to be, far from the job you were meant to be doing, far from the God you were meant to serve.

*

But there's got to be more to it than that. Even if I am an establishment professional, serene on the surface and a cauldron beneath, there has to be more to it than that. There are plenty of people who are like me. There has to be more to it than that.

And there was. Ezekiel needed a catalyst to bring it to a head. And he had it. More to the point, *it* had *him.* Something happened to him over which he had *no* control, just as he had had no control over everything that he was. His age, no control. His parents, no control. His country, no control. His religion, no control. His job, no control.[4] His exile, no control. The political mess, no control. The religious mess, no control. He was given his life. He was given his country. He was given his religion. He was given his job. He was given his brains to do his job. He was given the rotten politics. He was given the rotten religion. He was thrown into exile. The Christian word for "grace" came from the root for "gift."

He needed a catalyst to bring it to a head. To show him that if he were ever to be found by God he would have to be lost by himself. To show him that his whole life was not a matter of what he had done but of what had been done to him. To show him that he was what he wasn't. That was how he would become a puppet. And, as so often in the Bible, it would be a common experience. Serendipity is of the usual.

Moses had a bush (Exod. 3:2). Amos had a plumb line (Amos 7:7). Isaiah had a chant (Isa. 6:3). Jeremiah had a boiling pot (Jer. 1:13). Jesus had John (Mark 1:9). Peter had a servant girl (Luke 22:56). Paul had Stephen and Ananias (Acts 22:20, 13). And Ezekiel had a thunderstorm.

> As I looked, behold, a stormy wind came out of the north, and a great cloud, with brightness round about it, and fire

flashing forth continually, and in the midst of the fire, as it were gleaming bronze (Ezek. 1:4).

That was what put it all together for Ezekiel.

And the hand of the Lord was upon him there (Ezek. 1:3).

What common experience, church member, put it together for you?

NOTES

1. W. Eichrodt, *Ezekiel* (Phila.: Westminster, 1970), p. 1.
2. H. G. May in *The Interpreter's Bible* (New York: Abingdon, 1956), vol. 6, p. 68.
3. C. G. Howie in *The Interpreter's Dictionary of the Bible* (New York: Abingdon, 1962), vol. 2., p. 209.
4. "He was a hereditary member of the priesthood." Eichrodt, *op. cit.*, p. 53.

7

THE POINT IS TO BE REDUCED

It is one thing to say, "The hand of the Lord was upon him there," as was said of Ezekiel (Ezek. 1:3). But how does the church member who is still hanging in there *know* it is the hand of the Lord? It could be the hand of fate. It could be the hand of intuition. It could be the hand of common sense. Plenty of people have things happen to them. Plenty of people experience thunderstorms. And they do not attribute their experiences to God. How does the church member know it is God?

I

᚛ *First,* you're shown something you never saw before. In Ezekiel's case it was the chariot. Your imagination is fired. "Imagination," Einstein said, "is more important than knowledge."[1]

> Now as I looked at the living creatures, I saw a wheel upon the earth beside the living creatures, one for each of the four of them. As for the appearance of the wheels and their construction: their appearance was like the gleaming of a chrysolite; and the four had the same likeness, their construction being as it were a wheel within a wheel (Ezek. 1:15–16).

What does this mean? It means that one of the ways a church member knows it might be God is if a powerful new reality has broken into his or her life. Yes, it is a vision. Yes, it is imaginative. Yes, it is mystical. You're shown something you never saw before. You don't see it. You're shown it. You had nothing to do with it. It is evidence that a new reality is breaking in on you. We all live in three dimensions—that of self, others, world. But we do not all live in the fourth dimension, God. When you are shown something you never saw before, when your imagination is stoked, when a powerful new reality breaks into your life, that is evidence that the fourth dimension is breaking in on you, is being *brokered* by your *church*.

No, it is not conclusive proof. We do not all have visions like Ezekiel's. But it is evidence. It does count. It does happen. And it can happen to anyone. Remember, Ezekiel was in position for the powerful new reality to grip him. The hand of the Lord was upon him there because of all the things that had happened to him. Not because of anything *he* had done, but because of all the things that had been done *to* him. Young, middle-class, professional, serene on the surface, a cauldron beneath.

OK, but come on, who ever sees a vision, even a little one? Forget the vision if that's not your style, and go with the new reality. The church member is shown something he never saw before. It all comes into focus. "I see it clearly now," you say. "Whatever I perceive as clear and distinct," Descartes said, "is true."[2] "For the first time in my life," you say, "the whole thing makes sense." It happens instantly. You have nothing to do with it. You're walking down the street, and it "hits" you. "All of a sudden." You turn and look and God was there. That is your thunderstorm. Grace is serendipity.

II

Second, the church member is told something he or she never heard before. In Ezekiel's case he was given his orders. His emotion was fired. "What our blood feels and believes and says," wrote D. H. Lawrence, "is always true."[3]

> Son of man, I send you to the people of Israel, to a nation of rebels, who have rebelled against me. . . . Son of man, all my words that I shall speak to you receive in your heart, and hear with your ears. And go, get you to the exiles, to your people, and say to them, "Thus says the Lord God" (Ezek. 2:3, 3:10–11).

What does that mean? It means that one of the ways you know it might be God is if a powerful new compulsion has broken into your life. Yes, it is "emotional." Yes, it is "irrational." Yes, it is "mystical." You're told something you never heard before, and it *could* be God.

God does not simply come out of hiding. He comes out of silence. He is not only in light, he is in sound. You don't just see clearly, you hear clearly. Your experience is not only imaginative, it is emotive. The vision is never an end in itself in the Hebrew-Christian tradition, as it is in the Hindu tradition. It is always a means to an end. You always move from vision to audition in the Bible. From what you see to what you hear. From what you are shown to what you are told. From sight to sound. From pictures to words.

"I've got this feeling," we say. "It's as though something were telling me to do something. As though I were being asked to do something. As though I were being *told* do do something." Whether or not we do it is, of course, a different matter. But the fact is we feel it. More accurately, the fact is we *hear* it.

No, we may not hear it as clearly and distinctly as Ezekiel, but that is not the point. It is a dodge to say that I cannot have a religious experience because I am not as imaginative and emotional as Ezekiel. The point is *he* was no more imaginative and emotional than we are. *He* didn't have a religious experience. The religious experience had *him.* That sounds mystical? Fine. That's not the way you run your life? Fine. The point is you *are* run. You *are* called. All the time. You're walking down the street and hear your name. The church's job is to shout.

III

Third, we're hurt. It isn't nice, but it has to be said because it is there. "First a poet's heart must break," wrote Kierkegaard.[4]

> The Spirit lifted me up and took me away, and I went in bitterness in the heat of my spirit, the hand of the Lord being strong upon me; and I came to the exiles at Tel-abib, who dwelt by the river Chebar. And I sat there overwhelmed among them seven days (Ezek. 3:14–15).

First there was the anguish of his body. He was paralyzed.[5] That is how he knew it was God. It was an epitome of the passive. He couldn't move. The only way he *could* move was to *be* moved by the Spirit.

> The Spirit entered into me and set me upon my feet (Ezek. 2:2).
>
> Then the Spirit lifted me up (Ezek. 3:12).
>
> The Spirit . . . took me away (Ezek. 3:14).

Then there was the anguish of his mind. He had a mental breakdown.[6] That was how he knew it was God. God *was* what broke down his ability to do it on his own. He *couldn't* do it on his own. It was too overpowering. "I sat there overwhelmed among them seven days." "He can only *break down* before the *glory* of heavenly *power* as it *forces* its way into him."[7]

No, you don't have to have a mental breakdown to be a church member, but you do have to be broken. What you are shown and what you are told must be so powerful that they break you. At last you, the vaunted middle-class professional, come up against something *you* cannot do. That is why church growth is not for everyone and why church growth is not the point.

No, you don't have to be paralyzed to be a church member, but you do have to be rendered powerless to move on your own. If you *could* do what you heard and say what you saw, then it wouldn't be God. It would still be you, and that wouldn't be enough. If it's that easy for you to move on your vision, that easy for you to move on your audition, then go back to the banks of the river Chebar because you haven't seen, you haven't heard. Not yet. You are not yet a church member.

Then there was the anguish of Ezekiel's spirit. He was hurt in his body. He was hurt in his mind. And he was hurt in his soul. Time after time after time he is addressed with a phrase used nowhere else in the Old Testament except one place which is derived from here.[8] It is a term of weakness. It is an epitome of the passive. It is the opposite of God. It means "born of dust."[9] *Ben adam.* "Son of man" (Ezek. 2:1 *et pas.*).

It was an attempt to reduce him. To put him in perspective. To mock his attempts at self-fulfillment. To mock his pretension. To mock his middle-class can-do bootstrap theology. "And you, O son of man, behold, cords will be placed upon you, and you shall be bound with them, so that you cannot go out among the people; and I will make your tongue cleave to the roof of your mouth, so that you shall be dumb" (Ezek. 3:25–26).

Is it any accident that this is the phrase, *ben adam,* son of man, that Jesus picked up and applied to himself (Matt. 8:20 *et pas.*), the suffering servant (Isa. 53), the humiliated one, the crucified one, the slave (Phil. 2:7)?

Yes, you do have to be spiritually broken before you can be spiritually whole. It is a law of religion. It is a law of church membership. "The sacrifice acceptable to God is a broken spirit" (Ps. 51:17). You have to be put in perspective. You have to be steamrollered. You have to be flattened. You have to be leveled before God. The hurt in your body and the hurt in your mind and the hurt in your soul have to reduce you to a *ben adam,* a son of man. That's why churches are losing members. People don't like to be leveled.

IV

You're shown something you never saw. You're told something you never heard. You're hurt. *Fourth,* you're sent. "Son of man, go, get you to the house of Israel, and speak with my words to them" (Ezek. 3:4).

The compulsion was overwhelming. He had to do it. He couldn't *not* do it and still be Ezekiel. He couldn't refuse because it would mean refusing his blood. The vision, the audition, the suffering had done their work.

Yes, you have to be shown something you never saw. Yes, you have to be told something you never heard. Yes, you have to be hurt. All these things have to happen *to* you if the one big thing is going to happen *through* you. If you are going to be so passive that you are paralyzed by the hand of God and the only way for you to move is to *be* moved.

First, it was what he did, this figurehead, this puppet. He did what he was told to do. The strings were pulled and he responded. He couldn't move apart from the strings. He was *paralyzed* apart from the strings. A church member is *nothing* apart from the strings. A church can do *nothing* on its own.

(John 15)

> Son of man, take a brick and lay it before you, and portray upon it a city, even Jerusalem; and put siegeworks against it, and build a siege wall against it, and cast up a mound against it; set camps also against it, and plant battering rams against it round about (Ezek. 4:1–3).

He was to draw a picture of a city under siege. It was Jerusalem. It was the way the prophets spoke. It was the way they got their message across. It was the way the vision became the audition and the audition became the commission. "Son of man, go." And he went. First with the passive acts called symbols.

They are what the church should be doing all the time. People scoff at churches which reach for one-to-one giving—a dollar to benevolences for every dollar for "operating." They call it crazy. They say, Take care of our own first. Fix the parking lot. Build the new education unit. Buy the new sanctuary. One-to-one giving is a symbolic act, and if we ever let up on that kind of symbolic action, then we are through as churches. People *leave* churches that draw those kinds of symbols. Excellent. They should leave.

The *job* of the church is to produce symbolic actions. No, that isn't the job of the church at all. The job of the church is to be *used* as an instrument *through* which symbolic actions can *be* done. No, they are not going to please everyone. No, they are not going to be easy. No, they are not going to succeed every time. But the *point* is that the church is one organization in society that is going to be hurt by what it sees and hurt by what it hears. And that out of that intense suffering, an anguish so unbearable that the church breaks down and can't move and is humiliated, ever new symbolic actions are born to meet the agony of our time.

Second, it was what Ezekiel said, this figurehead, this puppet. He said what he was *told* to say. The voice spoke *through* him. He was *nothing* apart from the voice. He couldn't speak apart from the voice. He was dumb apart from the voice. It couldn't be put more graphically:

> "Son of man . . . open your mouth, and eat what I give you." And when I looked, behold, a hand was stretched out to me, and, lo, a written scroll was in it; and he spread it before me; and it had writing on the front and on the back, and there were written on it words of lamentation and mourning and woe. And he said to me, "Son of man, eat what is offered to you; eat this scroll, and go, speak to the house of Israel" (Ezek. 2:3, 8b–3:1).

And what did he say? What is the church *told* to say? Come off your inveterate nationalism. It is no good. You want to be master. It is the opposite of the slave. It is the opposite of the suffering servant. It is the opposite of the crucified one. It is the opposite of being used by me for my purposes. It is the opposite of humiliation. It is the opposite of reduction. They were more interested in national self-aggrandizement than they were in international justice. And the middle-class establishment which ran the businesses, ran the churches, ran the government was more interested in its tax breaks and profit margins than it was in domestic justice.

> Son of man, prophesy against the shepherds of Israel, prophesy, and say to them, even to the shepherds, Thus says the Lord God: Ho, shepherds of Israel who have been feeding yourselves! Should not shepherds feed the sheep? You eat the fat, you clothe yourselves with the wool, you slaughter the fatlings; but you do not feed the sheep. The weak you have not strengthened, the sick you have not healed, the crippled you have not bound up, the strayed you have not brought back, the lost you have not sought, and with force and harshness you have ruled them (Ezek. 34:2–4).

Of course his own kind were against him. Of course he was a "traitor to his class." Of course they wanted to get rid of him. Of course the church should shut up about social issues and about its *own* self-aggrandizement. Of course the church should say nothing about low-income housing in our golden ghettos. It made no difference. After all that he had already suffered in body, mind, and soul, it made no difference. "Son of man . . . whether they hear or refuse to hear . . . they will know that there has been a prophet among them" (Ezek. 2:3, 5).

*

But that was not all. It was not simply a word of judgment; it was a word of hope. That is what churches, of all institutions, are charged to bring. The hand of the Lord is upon them to do that. If they don't do it, then the hand of the Lord is not upon them. They are charged with the word of life. The word of change. The word of renewal. The word of hope.

He gave them his own visions. Give us a vision, the world is crying to the church. The visions were given through him. There was the vision of the valley of dry bones (Ezek. 37). It kindled hope.

> I will bring you home into the land of Israel. . . . I will put my Spirit within you, and you shall live (Ezek. 37:12, 14).

He gave them the vision of the river of life (Ezek. 47).

> And wherever the river goes every living creature which swarms will live (Ezek. 47:9).

He gave them the vision of their own city, a giant no more.

> And the name of the city henceforth shall be, [Yahweh-shammah] The Lord is there (Ezek. 48:35).

He gave them the vision of a new life.

> A new heart I will give you, and a new spirit I will put within you; . . . and I will be your God (Ezek. 36:26, 28).

He gave them the vision of the shepherd who cares for his sheep.

> For thus says the Lord God: Behold, I, I myself will search for my sheep, and will seek them out. . . . And I will feed them on the mountains of Israel, by the fountains, and in all the inhabited places of the country. I will feed them with good pasture, and upon the mountain heights of Israel shall be their pasture; there they shall lie down in good grazing land, and on fat pasture they shall feed on the mountains of Israel (Ezek. 34:11, 13–14).

Shown. Told. Hurt. Sent. "And the hand of the Lord was upon him there." That's the church.

NOTES

1. Einstein, quoted in *Reader's Digest,* May 1970.
2. Descartes, in A. Castell, *An Introduction to Modern Philosophy* (New York: Macmillan, 1943), p. 105.
3. D. H. Lawrence, quoted in *New York Times Book Review,* 18 March 1962.
4. S. Kierkegaard, *Journals* (London: Oxford, 1951), p. 397.
5. W. Eichrodt, *Ezekiel* (Phila.: Westminster, 1970), p. 25.
6. *Ibid.,* p. 72.
7. *Idem.,* ital. add.
8. *Ibid.,* p. 61.
9. *Ibid.,* p. 71.

8

THE POINT IS TO PREACH

It is one thing to say God must happen. It is another thing to say God has happened. It is still another thing to tell how God happened to you. It is this telling that is one of the passive acts of faith. It goes by the name of evangelism or witnessing, or simply, preaching. And it is *required* of church members. "Woe to me," Paul said, "if I do not preach the gospel!" (1 Cor. 9:16). The point, therefore, is to leave the church if you won't preach and to stay if you will.

Preaching shares with the other passive acts certain characteristics which make the action passive rather than active. It is to be remembered, however, that a passive act is just that, an act. The passive person always acts. The active person is not always passive. It is a big difference. When a person is active, big things can be done by him. When a person is passive, bigger things will be done through him.

I

The *first* thing to be said about preaching is that the church member doesn't *want* to do it. It's not his or her thing. A passive action is *never* your thing. It is never in your self-interest. It is never something you want to do. It is never something you would

61

do if it were left to you to do it. It is always something you want to avoid. It is always something you want to resist. It is always something that isn't you at all.

Moses, refusing to preach (Exod. 4:10). Jeremiah, refusing to preach (Jer. 1:6). Jonah, refusing to preach; indeed, being so averse to telling how God had happened to him that he fled. Paul, refusing to preach; indeed, being so averse to telling how God had happened to him that he jailed and even killed people who did tell.

Nobody wants to preach. They were no different from anybody else. It wasn't their thing; it isn't ours. They resisted; we resist. They avoided; we avoid. It wasn't them; it isn't us. Ninety-five percent of us, according to one estimate, have so resisted the passive act of preaching that we have not won a single other person for Christ.[1]

And yet they preached. The power of the passive was so great that they did what they didn't want to do. They were spun around. They did a complete about-face. Only *they* didn't do it. That was the point. They *were* spun. They *were* turned around. They *were* commissioned. They *were* sent. "Go . . . and make disciples of all nations" (Matt. 28:19). It wasn't their thing; but they did it. "As the Father has sent me, even so I send you" (John 20:21). They didn't want to go, but they went. "Those who were scattered went about preaching the word" (Acts 8:4). It was unbelievable, but it was happening. It was the church.

All the way back through the history of the passive it was happening. The power of the passive was that great. Plain, average, ordinary people were doing what they didn't want to do. They were doing what was not in their self-interest. They were doing what they resisted doing. They were doing precisely what they preferred not to be doing. They were doing precisely the thing that was not their thing.

A businessman:

> The Lord God has spoken;
> who can but prophesy?
> (Amos 3:8)

A laborer:

> Let my people go, . . . Let my people go, . . . Let my people go (Exod. 5:1, 8:1, 20 *et pas.*).
>
> Fear not, stand firm, and see the salvation of the Lord (Exod. 14:13).

A teenager:

> Then the Lord put forth his hand and touched my mouth; and the Lord said to me, "Behold, I have put my words in your mouth." (Jer. 1:9.)

A part-owner of a fishing business:

> Men of Judea and all who dwell in Jerusalem, let this be known to you, and give ear to my words (Acts 2:14).

A member of the upper-middle class, the same who had jailed and killed those who preached:

> Woe to me if I do not preach the gospel! (1 Cor. 9:16).
>
> I am under obligation (Rom. 1:14).
>
> We are ambassadors for Christ, God making his appeal through us (2 Cor. 5:20).

What had happened? *God* had happened. God *was* what turned them around. God *was* what sent them. God *was* what made them do what they didn't want to do. Yes, made them. Forced them. Used them. "He is a chosen instrument of mine," God said of the accomplice (Acts 9:15). "Necessity is laid upon me," said the accomplice himself (1 Cor. 9:16). He *had* to preach. "Woe to me if I do *not* preach!" He had no choice. It was a *passive* act. It wasn't his thing. It wasn't in his self-interest. Now *he* would be hunted. *He* would be killed, but he was *doing* it. A passive action is something you don't want to do, but you *are* doing it. We don't want to preach, but we find ourselves preaching. That *proves* God. It has to be God because *we* don't want any part of it, and yet we *are* preaching. We find ourselves doing precisely what we do not want to do. That *is* God because it *can't* be us. When it can't be us, it is the church.

II

Which leads to a *second* characteristic of passive acts. First, we have no choice. Second, we have no chance. We won't do it, and we *can't* do it. We do not want to do it, and we are unable to do it. It is beyond us. It is out of the question. It is impossible. "With men," Jesus said, "it *is* impossible" (Mark 10:27).

It is not simply a matter of church members not wanting to preach. It is a matter of not being *able* to preach. We don't have the equipment. We don't have the personality. We don't have the voice; we don't have the words; we don't have the enthusiasm. "Oh, my Lord, I am not eloquent," the laborer pleaded. " . . . I am slow of speech and of tongue" (Exod. 4:10). But it didn't matter. It had nothing to do with anything. Of *course* Moses could not speak. Nobody ever said he could speak. It was irrelevant. It was completely beside the point. It didn't matter. What did matter was that God could speak and that he would speak through Moses.

> Who has made man's mouth? Who makes him dumb, or deaf, or seeing, or blind? Is it not I, the Lord? Now therefore go, and *I* will be with your mouth and teach you what you shall speak (Exod. 4:11–12).

God *was* what enabled Moses to speak. God *was* what forced him to preach. Yes, forced. God *was* what he said because obviously *he* could not say it. He didn't have the equipment. Therefore it *must* be God. God *is* what enables us to talk about God. God *is* what enables us to tell how God has happened. God *is* what makes preaching possible.

We won't do it, and we can't do it. We have no choice, and we have no chance. Preaching is a passive act. Of course church members can't do it. That is the point of passive acts. God is what does it, not us. That is the point. It is done through us, not by us. We cannot do it. That is the point. If we could do it, it wouldn't be God. "With men it is impossible, but not with God." It has to be God because it obviously can't be us. Left to our own devices we wouldn't do it. Left to our own devices we couldn't do it.

Ah, but why all the talk about church members? Moses was three thousand years ago. It happened then, but it doesn't happen now. Amos, Jeremiah, Jonah, Peter, Paul. They obviously had pipelines to God. That is the point of the Bible. It collects the stories of the few men and the few women who *were* able to preach. But that kind of preaching doesn't happen any more.

No, that is precisely *not* the point of the Bible. Again, the people in the Bible are distinguished by nothing so much as their ordinariness. Yes, they were businessmen. Yes, they were laborers. Yes, they were housewives. Yes, they were teenagers. They were plain, average, ordinary, everyday people like us. It is a dodge to say it could happen then but it cannot happen now. It is a cop-out to say they could preach then but we cannot preach now. And it is not only a cop-out, it is historically inaccurate. Churches exist today because church members kept the preaching going. Everyday people like us kept the preaching going in A.D. 50. "Those who were scattered went about preaching the word." You bet they did, and that is why the church exists. "Woe to me if I do not preach the gospel!"

But what about that special class of people called "preachers"? Are not they the ones responsible for keeping the message of

Jesus current and hot? No. Don't we pay them to do that? No. It is incredible how backwards we have let things become in our churches. None of the first preachers was a clergyman. Not Moses, not Amos, not Jeremiah, not Jonah, not Peter, not Paul. None of the disciples was a clergyman. Jesus was not a clergyman. Preaching was public.[2] It was to non-Christians by nonclergymen. It was to those who had not yet heard it. Teaching was to Christians. Jesus preached to the crowds and taught the disciples. There is hardly any preaching in churches on Sunday morning. It is virtually all teaching. The *congregation* are the preachers. *"We* are ambassadors for Christ, God making his appeal through *us"* (2 Cor. 5:20). "Those who were scattered went about preaching the word." The clergyman may be an assistant coach, but the congregation is the team. The clergyman's sole job is to remind them that they are the team. And it is to do so by helping them to be steamrollered by the passive. Yes, steamrollered. Roger Staubach did not call one play in the '72 Super Bowl. Every play was sent in. If you have to call the plays, then the church is not for you.

This is why the image we have of church members is that of slaves (Rom. 1:1 *et pas.*). It fits the passive. Obviously the slave didn't want to be a slave, but he *was* a slave. Obviously the slave could do nothing on his own. He could only do what he was told to do. All he could do was take orders. All he could do was obey. He had no choice, and he had no chance—not on his own. And that meant that all he could do was take what was coming to him. As we have seen, God steamrollered Paul, flattening him by the side of the road. He told him through a preacher that he was an instrument, which Paul later translated as slave. And then he told him through the same preacher: "I will show him how much he must suffer for the sake of my name" (Acts 9:16). All the church member can do, since it is being done through him not by him, is take what is coming to him. And Paul took a lot:

> Five times I have received . . . the forty lashes less one. Three times I have been beaten with rods; once I was stoned.

> Three times I have been shipwrecked; a night and a day I
> have been adrift at sea; . . . in hunger and thirst, often
> without food, in cold and exposure (2 Cor. 11:24, 25, 27).

That is what happens to us when we can't do it. We can expect
trouble. Why? Because we are not in control. "The love of
Christ," Paul gasped, "controls *us*" (2 Cor. 5:14). Obviously if we
were in control, we would control our trouble. We would either
eliminate it or keep the lid on it. But when you are being used,
when you are being forced, when you are being manipulated,
when all the plays are being made through you not by you, then
you can expect all sorts of trouble from your preaching, as well
as what Paul called the "fruits of the Spirit," namely "love, joy,
peace" (Gal. 5:22).

III

Which leads to a *third* characteristic of passive acts. We get *no
credit.* It is almost as though our trouble were reducing us to size.
We won't do it. We can't do it. And we get no credit when it is
done through us not by us. All credit goes to the master, none
to the slave. All to the Christ, none to the church. It is *his* plan,
his work, *his* action, and he is *using* us. Yes, using. It is almost as
though the things that happen to church members were trying to
drop them, us, out of sight. It is as though we were vanishing.
What is your vanishing point? "What we preach," Paul said, "is
not ourselves, but Jesus Christ" (2 Cor. 4:5). The preacher is
"nothing" (2 Cor. 12:11). It is the word Paul used. It was the
ultimate in passive action. The actor had vanished. He was no
more. You saw not the preacher but the preached, not the actor
but the Christ. "*He* must increase," John the Baptist said of
Christ in the perfect preacher's motto, "but *I* must decrease"
(John 3:30).

It is for this reason that the passive actor can claim no credit.
"If I preach the gospel, that gives me *no* ground for boasting. For

necessity is laid upon me. Woe to me if I do *not* preach the gospel!" He didn't want to do it. He couldn't do it. But since he was doing it, he insisted that *he* get no credit. There is no end to the good you can do, it has been said, if you don't care who gets the credit. *No* credit is due the passive actor. He has simply done what he was told to do. "When you have done all that is commanded you," Jesus said, "say, 'We are *un*worthy servants; we have only done what was our *duty*'" (Luke 17:10).

The passive actor gets *no* credit. He can make *no* claim on God. Churches simply do their jobs. They do what they are employed to do. The slave works all day in the field in Jesus' illustration, and the master feels under *no* obligation even to thank him, much less to pay him. We cannot put God in our debt. Rewards are given because they are given, *not* because they are deserved. Israel deserved nothing and got everything. Paul deserved nothing and got everything. There is no room for pride. There is no room for merit. There is no room for credit. There is no room for reward. That is the point of church membership.

But there *is* room for power. "It is the power of God," Paul exclaimed of his preaching (1 Cor. 1:18). The power of the passive is enormous. One man gets twelve. The twelve become eleven. The man goes. The eleven scatter. They don't want it. They can't do it. And they certainly get no credit. They are cursed. They are beaten. They are stoned. They are shipwrecked. They are jailed. They are killed. And, as an angry crowd to whom they had preached said, "[They] have turned the world upside down" (Acts 17:6). That's the church.

NOTES

1. Quoted in D. James Kennedy, *Evangelism Explosion* (Wheaton, Ill.: Tyndale, 1971), p. 148.
2. P. H. Menoud in *The Interpreter's Dictionary of the Bible* (New York: Abingdon, 1962), vol. 3, p. 868–869.

9

THE POINT IS TO CREATE

I

Most churches cherish the illusion that their creativity springs from themselves. That they are responsible for it. That they produce creative relationships. That they produce creative policies. That they even produce creative art.

Nothing could be further from the truth as far as the Bible is concerned. The central thesis of the Bible is that *all* creativity is derivative. That when I am in creative relationship it is not I who have produced the relationship. That when I am creative institutionally it is not I who do the creating. That when I express myself creatively it is not I who do the expressing.

The classic statement of this thesis is Jeremiah's story of the potter and the pot. He felt impelled to go down to the potter's house. It was the objective pushing him. There he saw the potter at work. It was reality coming at him. And what he saw was a vessel spoiled, smashed, and then reworked. It was God and the Hebrew people.

The point is not that God is an artist. That is a word the translators specifically eschewed.[1] He is never called a demiurge in the Bible as he was by the Greeks. Rather the point is that God is a king. He is a ruler who has the power to bring into being what he wants to bring into being. Thus the end of creation is not an object of beauty but the subject of power. The thing created points not to itself in its beauty but to God in his power.

69

The Hebrew people are nothing apart from God. They are everything with him. They have significance only as they point beyond themselves to their creator. It is the same with the church. The pot has *no* significance apart from the potter. It wouldn't even *exist* apart from the potter. Its job is to do *whatever* the potter wants it to do. "Behold, like the clay in the potter's hand, so are you in my hand, O house of Israel" (Jer. 18:6).

*

Such a position has, of course, a number of logical consequences. One is that you worshiped the very thing you feared. No, it was not illogical, and it was certainly not inconsequential. You were drawn to what repelled you. You were pulled by what pushed you. It is the systole and diastole of creation. It had nothing whatever to do with what was created, but everything to do with the creator. It had nothing to do with us, in other words, but everything to do with God. God *is* what enables churches to create, but we do not praise what we create. We praise the God who enables us to create. We don't praise the product; we praise the process. And beyond the process we praise the producer. God is the creator, not the church. Michelangelo smashed his last statue because he felt it was so good it pointed to him and not to God. It was an object of beauty and no longer the subject of power.

> It is *I* who by my great power and my outstretched arm have made the earth, with the men and animals that are on the earth, and *I* give it to whomever it seems right to *me* (Jer. 27:5).

> Behold, *I* have created the smith
>   who blows the fire of coals,
>   and produces a weapon for its purpose.
> *I* have also created the ravager to destroy.
>   (Isa. 54:16)

> Be glad and rejoice for ever
> in that which *I* create.
>
> (Isa. 65:18)

> Praise him . . .
> Praise him . . .
> Praise him . . .
>
> (Ps. 150:3–5)

*

Still another consequence of the potter and his pot is that creation continues. The only constant for churches is change. The power is such that creation never stops. The word for "spirit" was the same as the word for "breath." "In the beginning God created . . . and the Spirit [or breath] of God was moving over the face of the waters" (Gen. 1:1–2).

> When thou sendest forth thy Spirit [or breath], they are created (Ps. 104:30).
>
> The wind [or spirit] blows where it wills (John 3:8).

Creation is as close as breathing. It is as constant. It is as powerful. It is as passive. We are not responsible for drawing our first breath. It is objective—a fact of life. It is real. Without it we die. Churches live to create. We create to live. We are in-spired. It means the "spirit within." God is breathing his creativity into us all the time. His mouth is on our mouths. His breath is our breath.

*

His words are our words. Uniquely the agent of creation is the word. "And God said" (Gen. 1:3). We will never know why. When God spoke, it was the moment of creation. "He commanded and they were created" (Ps. 148:5). Perhaps it was because when people spoke they revealed themselves. They created something between them. It was the way you could most reveal yourself, and it was available to all. You didn't have to be an artist. You didn't have to be a king. All you had to do was be yourself, and you too could create.

But there was more to it than that. In the Hebrew the word for "hear" meant to "obey." You did what you heard God say. God *was* what you did. God *was* what you created. That is not all God was, but God was at least that. Creation was obedience. The church were "slaves." The pot obeyed the hands of the potter, or it was not a pot. "He spoke, and it came to be; he commanded, and it stood forth" (Ps. 33:9).

II

Only it didn't. And this was where the trouble began. The pot wanted to be the potter. The creation wanted to be the creator. The people of Israel wanted to take the place of God. Churches want total responsibility for the product and the process. We want to be the producer. It is our building, our budget, our preaching, our witness.

> You turn things upside down!
>   Shall the potter be regarded as the clay;
> that the thing made should say of its maker,
>   "He did not make me";
> or the thing formed say of him who formed it,
>   "He has no understanding"?
>
>   (Isa. 29:16)

The creative process is destroyed by the product because the product won't let the process alone. They couldn't understand it, but it was happening all the time. We won't obey. We won't be used. We won't be formed. We won't *be* created. We *must* create.

> The ox knows its owner, . . . but Israel does not know [its]
> (Isa. 1:3).

What was the matter?

> He looked for it to yield grapes, but it yielded wild grapes
> (Isa. 5:2).

What was going on?

> The vessel he was making of clay was spoiled in the potter's
> hand (Jer. 18:4).

Why? Because

> we will follow our *own* plans (Jer. 18:12).

They refused to *be* planned. They refused to *be* used. They refused to be passive—clay in the hands of the potter. Virtually every church in America wants to do it the way they, we, want to do it.

So the fight was on—between the creator and the would-be creator—because the creator wouldn't stand for this. And the creative process to this day is a fight between whether we are doing it or whether it is being done through us.

> "Woe to him who strives with his Maker,
>   an earthen vessel with the potter!
> Does the clay say to him who fashions it, 'What are you making'?
>   or 'Your work has no handles'? . . .
> *I* made the earth,
>   and created man upon it;
> it was *my* hands that stretched out the heavens,
>   and *I* commanded all their host.
> *I* have aroused him in righteousness,
>   and *I* will make straight all his ways;
> he shall build *my* city

and set *my* exiles free,
not for price or reward,"
says the Lord of hosts.
(Isa. 45:9, 12–13)

But just as creation is constant so is the fight to be the creator constant. "Come, let us build ourselves a city, and a tower with its top in the heavens, and let us make a name for ourselves" (Gen. 11:4). Indeed, the pot was so flawed, the rebellion so constant, the creative process so upside down, that the Bible writers *give up hope* that we can be brought to our senses on our own. "Every imagination of the thoughts of his heart was only evil continually" (Gen. 6:5). "The imagination of man's heart is evil from his youth" (Gen. 8:21). The imagination—where the creative process takes place. "The heart is deceitful above all things, and desperately corrupt" (Jer. 17:9).

We have to *be* saved. We have to *be* rescued. Because we will *always*, as Paul says, "exchange the truth about God for a lie and worship and serve the creature rather than the Creator" (Rom. 1:25). It is in the human condition. He even says it was *put* in the human condition. *"God* has consigned all men to disobedience, that he may have mercy upon all" (Rom. 11:32). It is a staggering thought—that even the rebellion was planned. That the creative process *had* to go awry. That all of us following our own plans was planned (Isa. 53:6), Jer. 18:12). That the potter deliberately spoiled his pot. That he *made* the church fail. Because it was the only way, the *only* way, that the pot would stay a pot and not try to become the potter. It had to be smashed. *Then* it could be "reworked into another vessel, as it seemed good to the potter to do" (Jer. 18:4).

III

He makes the church. He breaks the church. He remakes the church. It is the rhythm of the creative life, and it too goes on,

because we always come back and back and back to try to displace
the creator. Indeed, it is one of the oldest myths in the history
of our race and is the background from which the Bible is written.[2] That creation is a battle with chaos, and that the only way
creation can take place is for the creator to beat and rebeat the
created.

> Thou didst crush Rahab like a carcass,
>> thou didst scatter thy enemies with they mighty arm.
> The heavens are thine, the earth also is thine;
>> the world and all that is in it, thou hast founded them.
>>>> (Ps. 89:10–11)

He makes us. He breaks us. He remakes us. The man who went
down to the potter's house saw it. He was that creative, that
caught up in the process, that stunned by the reality and objectivity of it.

> I will make a new covenant with the house of Israel and the
> house of Judah, . . . and I will write it upon their hearts; and
> I will be their God, and they shall be my people. . . . for I
> will forgive their iniquity, and I will remember their sin no
> more (Jer. 31:31, 33–34).

Others saw it. "A new heart I will give you," wrote the phenome-
nally creative Ezekiel, "and a new spirit I will put within you"
(Ezek. 36:26).

> How can I give you up, O Ephraim [cried the
>> imaginative Hosea]!
> How can I hand you over, O Israel! . . .
> My heart recoils within me,
>> my compassion grows warm and tender.
>>>> (Hos. 11:8)

But these words, powerful as they were, were not powerful
enough. The way God would do it would be through a single

individual—broken and then remade. It would have to be some-body who knew that he had no power on his own. Who knew that the key to creativity was having it done through him not by him. Who knew that his freedom lay in slavery and that the only way he could freely create was slavishly to obey.

> Truly, truly, I say to you, the Son can do *nothing* of his own accord (John 5:19).
>
> The Father who dwells in me does *his* works (John 14:10).
>
> [He] emptied himself, taking the form of a slave, . . . and became obedient unto death (Phil. 2:7–8).

For many people, the way to be creative now lay in their rela-tionship to him. If somehow they could be "in Christ," they could be endlessly creative. They could *be* a church. Indeed, one of them was so dumbfounded by the possibility that he said, "If any one is in Christ, he is a new creation; the old has passed away, behold, the new has come" (2 Cor. 5:17). It was as dramatic as the first creation. They even used the imagery from it. They even called him "the Word" (John 1:1). "It is the God who said, 'Let light shine out of darkness,' who has shone in our hearts to give the light of the knowledge of the glory of God in the face of Christ" (2 Cor. 4:6).

Again, what were the consequences? For one thing creation was by God. That had been recovered. "We are his workman-ship" (Eph. 2:10). "All this is from God" (2 Cor. 5:18). They did nothing to deserve it. They got no credit. The potter had simply remade his pot. It was objective. It was real. It was the church.

And it came to them through Christ. "All this is from God, who through Christ reconciled us to himself" (2 Cor. 5:18). And what a reconciliation. What a remaking. What extraordinary creativity was now released. The product was being used. Listen to a stunned church member. "I have been crucified with Christ; it is no longer *I* who live, but Christ who lives in *me;* and the life I now live in the flesh I live by faith in the Son of God, who loved *me* and gave himself for *me*" (Gal. 2:20). It was unbelievable, but it was endlessly creative. Are we saved by creativity? No, we are saved by the God who makes us endlessly creative.

So creative that the process continues through us. Yes, it is hard to imagine. But yes, it happens. "So we are ambassadors for Christ, God making his appeal *through us*" (2 Cor. 5:20). The church begins with God and ends broken and remade. It is the opposite of our usual thinking about the creative process. Things *are* upside down, but they work; they create. And that means they matter. "Through *you* I vindicate *my* holiness before their eyes" (Ezek. 36:23). The church is aligned with the theorhythms of the universe. Its creativity is derivative. Church members point, not to what they have made in its beauty, but to the one who is constantly remaking them in his power.

NOTES

1. W. Foerster in G. Kittel, *Theological Dictionary of the New Testament* (Ann Arbor, Mich.: Eerdmans, 1965), vol. 3, p. 1024.
2. *Ibid.*, p. 1009.

10

THE POINT IS TO PRAY

The passive acts, as we have seen, are the ones that are done through us not by us. They are where the power is. And certainly the most familiar, and perhaps the most available, is the passive act of prayer.

I

Prayer begins in objectivity. Something happens to us. It is more than we can handle. It may be either negative or positive. Our response is our prayer. We go outside our experience to understand what is happening inside our experience.

This means that the object of prayer may be anything. It all depends upon how much the church member is affected. And that, of course, depends on how affectable he or she is. How sensitive. How impressionable. How alert.

It is a truism to say that most of us slide through life. Things are happening to us all the time, but we don't let them affect us. "Pray constantly," Paul said (1 Thess. 5:17), but he was impressionable. He let things affect him. "In everything," he said, "by prayer and supplication with thanksgiving let your requests be made known to God" (Phil. 4:6).

But there was more to it than that. The objective did its work

78

with more power. You *had* to pray because what was happening to you was so powerful you were *forced* to pray to understand it. Not everyone, of course, but certainly person after person in the Hebrew-Christian tradition.

Take Jesus. We assume, because he was impressionable, that he prayed in the synagogue, prayed at meals, and so on.[1] But when he really prayed was either before, during, or after the big events of his life. Something was happening to him, and he *had* to pray in order to understand it. The objective was coming at him that hard.

According to Mark, our earliest source, Jesus prayed before he announced his preaching tour (Mark 1:35) and after feeding the multitude (Mark 6:46). He prayed before he appointed the twelve (Mark 3:13), after they returned from their mission (Mark 6:32), and before his transfiguration (Mark 9:2). Big things were happening to him, and in order to understand them he had to pray.

But there was even more to it than that. The objective did its work with even more power. It was the biggest things that forced him to pray the most. There are only two actual prayers of Jesus recorded in this earliest source. Both are from the most difficult and un-understandable time in his life. The first before the crucifixion (Mark 14:36) and the second during the crucifixion (Mark 15:34).

> Abba, Father, . . . remove this cup from me.
>
> My God, my God, why hast thou forsaken me?

In other words, prayer is not just a matter of what happens to church members, impressionable as they may be. It is not just a matter of the big events in our lives, powerful as they may be. Prayer is a matter of crisis, of the biggest events, of the things that are happening to us that we understand the least and that pound us the most. The deepest prayer occurs when you feel yourself leveled by circumstance, out of control, passive before the on-slaught of the objective. When you feel that the only thing you can do is pray. That the only way out is to pray. That you *have* to pray or you can't go on.

Stephen is being killed, and he prays (Acts 7:55). Paul and Silas are in prison, and they pray (Acts 16:25). Jeremiah is hounded by the establishment, and he prays (Jer. 20:7). Hannah is overcome, and she prays (1 Sam. 1:10). The people of Israel are in deep trouble, and they pray (Judg. 3:9). The psalmist feels forsaken, and he prays.

> My God, my God, why hast thou forsaken me?
>   Why art thou so far from helping me, from the words of my
>   groaning?
> O my God, I cry by day, but thou dost not answer;
>   and by night, but find no rest.
>
>   (Ps. 22:1–2)

This was the heart of the matter. Not only that they were in crisis. Not only that they were out of control. Not only that they could not understand. But that they were not *understood.* They felt abandoned, alone. That was where the terror was—that God had left them. All they wanted was God, and God was not there. They could handle anything with God. God *was* what enabled them to go on, but *God was not there.* The objective had *gone.* That is why people leave churches.

> Oh, that I knew where I might find him,
>   that I might come even to his seat! . . .
> Behold, I go forward, but he is not there;
>   and backward, but I cannot perceive him;
> on the left hand I seek him, but I cannot behold him;
>   I turn to the right hand, but I cannot see him.
>
>   (Job 23:3, 8–9)

II

But that is not where prayer ends. The passive act is so power-ful that it goes on. The circumstance may have leveled the person who prays, and he or she may feel abandoned by God. But the extraordinary thing is that the power of the passive act is such that the person who prays begins to feel that God was in the leveling. That God *was there all along.* That maybe even God *was* what brought the crisis in order that the person could be brought to God. Churches exist to foment crisis. It isn't popular.

Certainly Jesus didn't choose the crucifixion. He opposed it. "Abba, Father, . . . remove this cup from me." It was an artificial, unnatural, objective crisis forced upon him by God. This was the way God was going to get his work done, and Jesus was going to be passive before it. No wonder he felt forsaken. "My God, my God, why hast thou forsaken me?" It was going to be done through him, not by him, and he felt alone, abandoned.

Certainly Stephen didn't choose to be stoned to death. It was an artificial, unnatural, objective crisis forced upon him by his church membership. But the point was not that the prayer left him feeling abandoned. The point was that the power of the passive act was such that it left him feeling the *opposite* of aban-doned. It left him feeling so *close* to God that he could handle *anything.* "He, full of the Holy Spirit, gazed into heaven and saw the glory of God, and Jesus standing at the right hand of God; and he said, "Behold, I see the heavens opened, and the Son of man standing at the right hand of God." . . . Then they cast him out of the city and stoned him" (Acts 7:55–56, 58).

It was the same with Jeremiah, the same with Hannah, the same with the people of Israel, the same with the psalmist. The power of the passive act was such that it propelled them beyond for-sakenness to acceptance, beyond abandonment to support, beyond distance to closeness.

> O my God, I cry by day, but thou dost not answer;
>   and by night, but find no rest.
> *Yet* thou art holy,
>   enthroned on the praises of Israel.
> In thee our fathers trusted;
>   they trusted, and thou didst deliver them.
> To thee they cried, and were saved;
>   in thee they trusted, and were not disappointed.
>   (Ps. 22:2–5)

First the church cries, but then it remembers. That is what happens in the passive act of prayer. And the biblical data state that the memory is *more* powerful than the cry. Is your abandonment the pattern of history?[2] Not if you are in the Hebrew-Christian tradition. It is just the opposite. That God so loved the world that he would *not* abandon it. That God *is* what does *not* abandon you in the darkest hours of your crisis. "Let the hours be silent," Emerson said, "so the centuries can speak."[3] The church's job is to stagger us with the memory.

> These things I *remember*,
>   as I pour out my soul:
> how I went with the throng,
>   and led them in procession to the house of God,
> with glad shouts and songs of thanksgiving,
>   a multitude keeping festival. . . .
>
> My soul is cast down within me,
>   therefore I *remember* thee
> from the land of Jordan and of Hermon,
>   from Mount Mizar.
>
> Hope in God.
>   (Ps. 42:4, 6, 11)

No, it is not certain. No, it is not easy. No, it is not inevitable. We don't feel abandoned and then accepted and then that's it.

The emotion is too deep, the crisis too grave. The psalmist had no sooner prayed "Yet thou art holy" than he was back to his ravaging self-doubt and sense of forsakenness:

> But I am a worm, and no man;
>> scorned by men, and despised by the people.
> All who see me mock at me, . . .
> "He committed his cause to the Lord; let him deliver him,
>> let him rescue him, for he delights in him!"
>
> (Ps. 22:6–8)

It is never cut and dried in the religious life. There is always this back-and-forthness. Always the despair in churches alternates with the hope. "All sunshine," goes an Arab proverb, "makes the desert."[4]

Therefore church members have to do more than remember their religious processions. They have to do more than remember their religious homeland. They have to do more even than remember God's mighty acts in the history of their fathers and their own history. We have to remember the fundamental fact of our faith, namely that we were *thrown* onto God from the beginning, that the passive was at work even then because we had *nothing* to do with our own lives. "Upon thee was I cast from my birth" (Ps. 22:10). And that the passive is at work in us now in a way so mysterious that we feel God is the agent of the very prayer itself. God *is* what gets us to pray: the crisis. And God *is* our response to the crisis: the prayer. Therefore no prayer is unanswered because the answer is already contained in the question. We wouldn't *be* praying if *God* were not praying with us. God *is* what levels us. God *is* what reminds us.

> God has sent the Spirit of his Son into our hearts, crying, "Abba! Father!" (Gal. 4:6).
>
> When we cry "Abba! Father!" It is the Spirit *himself* bearing witness with our spirit (Rom. 8:15–16).

> We do not know how to pray as we ought, but the Spirit *himself* intercedes for us with signs too deep for words (Rom. 8:26).

> Your Father knows what you need before you ask him (Matt. 6:8).

Prayer *cannot* be unanswered. If it seems unanswered, then we haven't been used by the passive enough. Perhaps we have been too active, as typical church members, and have wanted to control the process when all along the process was trying to control us. "Prayer is *not* initiated entirely by man but depends ultimately on a *prior* activity of God."[5] That is what gives it its power. And when that is remembered, *all* prayer is answered. Maybe not the way we wanted it answered. Remember: Jesus asked that his cup of suffering be removed. But *always* answered. "The distinctive feature of early Christian prayer is the certainty of being heard."[6] Or, as Jesus put it: *"Whatever* you ask in prayer, believe that you receive it, and you *will"* (Mark 11:24).

III

But you cannot contain the passive act even there. It is too powerful. Yes, there was power in the cry. Yes, there was power in the memory. But there is also power for churches in the third act, namely, what they do after they pray.

Here is where the real power is because it is so obviously not we who are doing it. It is one thing to respond to a crisis. It is another thing to remember. But it is still another thing to do something because of the response and because of the memory.

Jesus went to the cross, but it was God not Jesus. He had broken through to the ultimate in prayer. He had broken through to the ultimate in power. "Abba, Father, all things are possible to thee; remove this cup from me; *yet not what I will, but what thou wilt.* " Obviously he couldn't do it. It would be done through him not by him. That was the point. That the power of prayer was such that he had been propelled beyond his cry and beyond his memory to the passive act of his own death for God.

"Not what I will, but what thou wilt." It is the key to the answering of prayer. We cry. We remember. We obey. Our power is our weakness. Our victory is our surrender. Our fulfillment is our annihilation. And, of course, very few people want to be annihilated, which is why they leave churches. "Three times I besought the Lord about this," Paul wrote describing his serious illness, " . . . but he said to me, 'My grace is sufficient for you, for my power is made perfect in weakness' " (2 Cor. 12:8–9).

Paul, the church member, did not get what he wanted, but he did get what God wanted. Yes, it seems incomprehensible that God wanted Paul to be sick. But that was the way Paul read it, and it gave him enormous power, not only to live with a possibly fatal illness, but the power to do what he felt God wanted him to do, what he had to do, throughout the Mediterranean world.

Or take Stephen, the one in whose death this same Paul had participated. Of course Stephen cried. Of course he remembered. It was his recounting of those memories of what God had done that got him into trouble. But we remember him most for what God did through him at the end. The power of the passive was so great, and the energy of his praying so compelling, that he did what Jesus did and prayed for those who were killing him: "Lord, do not hold this sin against them" (Acts 7:60).

Jeremiah, Hannah, the people of Israel, the psalmists—all were able to do what they never thought they could. The power of the passive was such that they broke through to "Not what I will, but what thou wilt." And that was *all* that mattered. It was the *point* of their religion. And it had nothing to do with the *growth* of the institution, except, of course, as a byproduct. If the institution grew because of prayer, fine. If it declined, equally fine. The point was to pray, not to grow.

The word for prayer in one of its forms comes from the phrase "to stroke the face of God."[7] The one who prays wants to be drawn that near to the force that determines his destiny. That remembers *him*. That cries for *him*. That uses *him*. He wants to be that close. And when he is that close, he can do anything. Anything, he feels, can be done through him. Stunned church members told how prayer could even heal (James 5:14, Acts 28:8). They told how it could even raise from the dead (Acts 9:40). Because out of their cries, out of their memories, and out of their willingness to be used they had reached out and stroked the face of God. He had come that close.

NOTES

1. C. W. F. Smith in *The Interpreter's Dictionary of the Bible* (New York: Abingdon, 1962), vol. 3, p. 862.
2. E. M. Poteat in *The Interpreter's Bible* (New York: Abingdon, 1955), vol. 4, p. 223.
3. *Idem.*
4. Poteat, *op. cit.*, p. 224.
5. Smith, *op. cit.*, p. 867 (ital. add.).
6. H. Greeven in G. Kittel, *Theological Dictionary of the New Testament* (Ann Arbor, Mich.: Eerdmans, 1963), vol. 2, p. 803 (ital. add.).
7. J. Hermann in H. Greeven, *op. cit.*, p. 785.

11

THE POINT IS TO BE FORGIVEN

I

Most church members don't yet have the power, and they want it. Or they have some and want more. Either way, it is one reason we belong to churches. Religion is power. That is not all religion is, but religion is at least that. It is the power to think. It is the power to feel. It is the power to act.

Now to be sure, a person can think, feel, and act without belonging to a church. What church membership offers is *more* thinking, *more* feeling, *more* acting. We belong to churches because we are greedy. We have thought, felt, and acted on many occasions. We have spent our entire lives thinking, feeling, acting. What we have not done is push to the limits of each. That is why we belong to churches.

Church membership offers the idea of God, which is a mind-expanding idea. It offers the experience of other people, which is an emotion-expanding feeling. And it offers doing something for and with those people, which is a motivation-expanding action.

To be specific, what church membership offers that you may not get anywhere else, and to be even more specific, what Christianity offers that you may not get in any other religion, is the thought-charged, emotion-laden, action-producing announcement, "You are forgiven."

At first blush that may not appear to be the life-enhancer it is.

We may not feel we need to be forgiven. Surely that is not why we joined a church. A poll was taken some years ago in which it was discovered that an astonishing 91 percent of us reported that we were honestly trying to lead a good life, although 82 percent of us admitted that the struggle was not interfering much with either our happiness or our enjoyment.[1]

Be that as it may, the fact is that the announcement is made through churches. It is one of the most stupendous announcements in the history of the world, and it is the most powerful single announcement in a church member's life.

You *are* forgiven. You are freed. You are released. It is the Good News of the gospel. The slate is wiped clean. You are given new life. You have the power. And you did *nothing* to deserve it. You *don't* deserve it. That is the *point* of forgiveness. If you deserved it, it wouldn't be forgiveness. You *are* forgiven.

It is a mind-expander. As a matter of fact, it was such a mind-expander that it met with violent opposition when it was first announced. "Why does this man speak thus?" the "church" people asked (Mark 2:7). "It is blasphemy! Who can forgive sins but God alone?" The people who were in the life-enhancing business were the very people most opposed to enhancing life.

The church buries its most important product. You *are* forgiven, but you wouldn't know it going to church on Sunday morning. Where's the joy? Where's the new life? Where's the thought, feeling, action? You *are* forgiven. Anything that gets in the way of the forgiveness must go. The job of the church is to announce the forgiveness. The message must get through. If it doesn't get through, then it isn't the church. We *are* forgiven, and if we leave church on Sunday morning not *knowing* that, then something is wrong with us or wrong with the church or wrong with both.

II

How does the message get through? *First,* there is the announcement itself. Preaching is a serious and miraculous business. Serious because the subject is nothing more or less than "new life" (2 Cor. 5:17). Miraculous because things begin to happen. One, the establishment takes offense. They were hostile to Jesus. They were hostile to the disciples. They will be hostile to you. If you aren't rejected, church member, then it isn't the gospel.[2] If church growth is going to decline, let's have it decline because members are being rejected for being offensive for Christ.

Two, you are the one doing the preaching. That is miracle enough right there, as we have seen. That's power. That's religion. Preaching was to nonbelievers,[3] and it was not limited to one class of people.

Three, the ideal is the real. Talk about mind-expanders. Talk about "realistic" budgets. Talk about "realistic" plans. In the preaching, what is being said *is* taking place. The ideal *is* the real. You *are* forgiven, and you begin to *experience* the forgiveness. "What is proclaimed is *actualized,*" writes an expert on early Christian preaching. "The word proclaimed is a *divine* Word, and as such it is an effective force which *creates what it proclaims.* Hence preaching is no mere interpretation of facts. It is event. What is proclaimed *takes place.*"[4]

The paralyzed man is forgiven. The woman who came to Jesus is forgiven (Luke 7:48). Zaccheus feels forgiven (Luke 19:1–10). It is unbelievable, but it's happening. In every instance the church people watching are outraged. Why? Because it was beyond belief that it should be happening. It was beyond belief that words could be that effective. It was beyond belief, yes; but it was not beyond behavior. It *was* happening. Even if it didn't fit into their scenario. Even if it didn't fit into their plans. Even if it was patently "unrealistic." It was the power of the passive.

Ah, but that was Jesus. Obviously he was effective, but he isn't around any more. Therefore the forgiveness is gone. Is it? What about the *church members* whom he specifically charged to go out there and preach forgiveness? "Then he said to them . . . that . . . forgiveness of sins should be preached in his name to all nations" (Luke 24:44, 47). What about them? Ineffective? Eleven. Seventy. The entire empire in three hundred years. Today one-third of the world. Nearly a billion people. Ineffective?

Something is going on in this word of forgiveness that is beyond our ability to describe, but is not beyond our ability to experience. It is announced—by him, by them, by us. Then it happens. It doesn't happen the other way around. That way it makes no sense. You don't believe your way to forgiveness. If you could, the scribes and Pharisees would have been forgiven long before anyone else. They were the professional believers. They were the keepers of the faith; but, as the parent who keeps the child too long, they were destroying what they loved the most. There was no room in their church plan for the "unrealistic" fact of forgiveness. They had closed themselves off from the very thing they wanted above everything else.

You don't believe your way to forgiveness; you believe your way *from* forgiveness. We don't believe it can happen. Why should it happen? Why should we be forgiven for what we have done? If anything, we shouldn't be forgiven. We should be punished.

We don't believe our way to forgiveness; we believe our way from forgiveness. It happens; then we believe it. The unbelievable thing is happening in us and through us and to us; then we believe it. That's the Good News. That it's happening. That it's happening to us. That we announce it.

III

And that it's happening *all the time.* That's the *second* way the message gets through. It's not only announced in a church service. It's not only announced through the people who are the church. It's not only announced through reading the Bible and prayer. It's being announced through all the events of our lives. That is how powerful the announcement is.

A man is sick; then the announcement comes. A woman comes to dinner; then the announcement comes. A man sees another man coming into town; then the announcement comes. The announcement of forgiveness is so powerful that it is not reserved for the big moments in a person's life. It can happen anytime, anywhere, anyhow. Grace, remember, is serendipity, and it is particularly serendipity of the usual. It is happening all the time, and it is happening regardless of what we do. It is that objective. It is that real. It is that powerful. It is that *passive.*

Zaccheus climbed the tree in *response* to the man who was coming into town. The woman came to dinner in *response* to the man who came to dinner. The paralyzed man came to the room in *response* to the man who came to the room. God is always coming at us in all the events of our lives. Grace is happening, but we don't expect it. Therefore we rule out 99 percent of everything that happens to us.

A mother and child stopped to see me. The child is two, and he carried in his hand a rock from the parking lot. He showed me the rock. We felt the rock. We dropped the rock. We had a geological conversation about the rock. It takes a two-year-old to put us back in touch with *reality.* We are that out of touch, that programmed, that planned, that nonpassive. Grace is what is happening to us that we didn't plan.

You can't plan God. That limits forgiveness to what is "realistic." But since forgiveness is obviously "unrealistic," we will never experience forgiveness. We have these elaborate plans in books on how to wake up the churches. But such plans are absurdly realistic. They limit the ideal to the real. They limit what we should do to what we could do. Who says the budget should increase 20 percent? That's ridiculous. Maybe the budget should increase 100 percent. Who says the membership should increase 10 percent? Maybe it should decrease.

God is coming at us *all the time,* and the only purpose of a plan is (a) to get us to fail and (b) to open us up to the 99 percent of everything we are closed off to. We have to drop it down to 98 percent, 97 percent, and so on to the point where we start hearing what God is saying and start responding to what God is doing. God *is* what is happening to us. That is not all God is, but God is at least that. And the most important thing we could be doing is opening ourselves up to the theorhythms of our lives.

IV

But, of course, *we* won't do it. It is too much for church members. Indeed, we *can't* do it. What opens us up *is* God in our lives. The divine is that powerful. We are that passive. Proof is not only our inability to feel forgiven, but our inability *to* forgive.

That is the *third* way the message gets through. It is announced through preaching. It is announced through the daily events of our lives. And it is announced through us—not by us, but through us. *We* forgive. Only we don't forgive. We *find* ourselves forgiving.

It is something *we* do not do. Left to ourselves we would not do it. It is as absurd to think we *are* forgiven as it is to imagine we *can* forgive. Not only do I not deserve to be forgiven, but neither does the other guy. So when I feel forgiven, it has to be God. And when I forgive, if I ever do, it has to be God, because it certainly couldn't be me. Left to my own devices, I wouldn't forgive. It is not my style. Somebody does me in, and I'm going to do him in. We don't forgive, but we find ourselves forgiving.

"Father, forgive them; for they know not what they do" (Luke 23:34). It has to be one of the most "transcendent" utterances of all time. It was obviously "beyond" his ability. You don't forgive your executioners while you are being executed. It couldn't be Jesus; it had to be God. That is what we mean when we say Jesus was divine. We mean that God was obvious because it couldn't be Jesus.

God *is* obvious when church members forgive. God *is* what enables us to forgive. That *is* God in your life. That is not all God is, but God is at least that. "Turn on the water! Loose the dogs! We ain't going back. Forgive them, O Lord."[5] It was the spiritual power of that forgiveness in Birmingham that helped our country think, feel, act better.

Jesus was insistent. You are forgiven; you must forgive. "Father, forgive them." Indeed, as we have seen, he went so far as to say, "If you do not forgive men their trespasses, neither will your Father forgive your trespasses" (Matt. 6:15). "How many times shall we forgive?" Peter asked. "Seven?" "Seventy times seven," Jesus replied (Matt. 18:22). And if you don't do it, he added, you ought to be tortured (Matt. 18:34). That's strong language for church members.

Angela Davis? The Berrigans? The young men who refused to serve in Vietnam? The young man who killed the babysitter and was released after only two years? Lieutenant Calley?

Left to our own devices we are not going to forgive those people, much less the people close to us in home, school, job, church. But we are *not* left to our own devices. That is the gospel. Not only that we *are* forgiven, but that we *can* forgive. And that God *is* the power to do both.

A man and his four friends were massacred on a sandbar in the remote Curaray River in the jungles of eastern Ecuador. Three years later the man's sister went to the primitive village where the killers lived. She announced God's forgiveness and her own, and she read to them from a book called "God's Carving," the Old Testament and the New.

Two years later four of the killers were baptized, and one year after, the fifth. "We didn't know they were coming to tell us about God," the killers said. "Now we understand. We are sorry we speared them. We'll go to our kinsmen downriver and read to them from God's carving. Then they too will walk on His trail."[6]

We *are* forgiven. We *can* forgive. That is the Good News. Those who announce it, those through whom it is announced, *are* the church.

NOTES

1. Paul Scherer in *The Interpreter's Bible* (New York: Abingdon, 1952), vol. 8, p. 325.
2. 1 Cor. 1:18, 23.
3. G. Friedrich in G. Kittel, *Theological Dictionary of the New Testament* (Grand Rapids, Mich.: Eerdmans, 1965), vol. 3, p. 713.
4. *Ibid.*, p. 711 (ital. add.).
5. Coretta Scott King, *My Life with Martin Luther King, Jr.* (New York: Avon, 1970), p. 235.
6. Minneapolis *Star*, 27 February 1971.

12

THE POINT IS TO BE INSPIRED

Granted that church membership may still be desirable, is it obtainable? How does it happen? How does it come? What is it that keeps people at it? What is it that causes me to do what I might not normally do? What is it that makes a church a church?

I

The spirit is the agent of the church. And the first thing to be said about the spirit is that it is elemental. When we talk about the spirit, we go back to our roots. Both in the ancient Greek and in the ancient Hebrew the word for spirit, as we have seen, was the word for breath.[1] The spirit was the breath of life, and that conception of it has stayed with us to this day. Whenever a person sneezes we say, "God bless you," so that his spirit, the breath of his life, which has just rushed from his body, will be caught by God and not, as the ancient superstition had it, by the devil.

> The spirit of God has made me,
>   and the breath of the Almighty gives me life.
> (Job 33:4)

> And when he had said this, he breathed on them, and said to them, "Receive the Holy Spirit" (John 20:22).

> Then the Lord God formed man of dust from the ground, and breathed into his nostrils the breath of life; and man became a living being (Gen. 2:7).

But the spirit is not only elemental, it is unpredictable. It is not only breath but wind.[2] And "The wind blows where it wills, and you hear the sound of it, but you do not know whence it comes or whither it goes; so it is with every one who is born of the Spirit" (John 3:8). Paul, unlikely, born of the spirit. Matthew, at the Internal Revenue, born of the spirit. Peter, part owner of a fishing business, born of the spirit. They proved that it could happen to anyone, and it did. Anyone could be a church member. "And they were *all* filled with the Holy Spirit" (Acts 2:4). That *was* what made them a church.

Elemental, unpredictable, and irresistible. Breath, wind, and storm. "Suddenly there came a sound from heaven like a violent blast of wind, which filled the whole house where they were seated" (Acts. 2:2, Moffatt). The spirit was power. It filled, gripped, seized the church member with elemental and unpredictable force.

> You shall receive *power* when the Holy Spirit has come upon you (Acts 1:8).

> The place in which they were gathered . . . was shaken; and they were all filled with the Holy Spirit. . . . And with great *power* [they] . . . gave their testimony (Acts 4:31, 33).

It was the root for energy.[3] The spirit was elementally dynamic. It was unpredictably vital. It was divinely powerful. That was the only way they could explain it. The energy was so great it could only be God.[4]"God *is* spirit" (John 4:24). If you haven't experienced the power, you may be "an active church member," but you are not yet an inspired one.

II

It is the power of the passive. You *are* seized. You *are* gripped. You *are* filled. You *are* overpowered. And *you* have nothing to do with it. It is not in your *power*. It is not in your control. It is not you, and it is not even *for* you. "It is not for *your* sake, O house of Israel, that I am about to act, but for the sake of *my* holy name" (Ezek. 36:22). That is how little the church has to do with whatever power it has. The church member is not the subject, but the object. Not the actor, but the acted upon. Not the doer, but the done-to. Not the elemental, unpredictable, irresistible activists we thought we were, but the in-spir-ed passivists.

It means "the spirit in." The breath in. The wind in. The storm in. You are inspired. You are possessed. You do not possess the spirit; the spirit possesses you. "The spirit of the Lord took possession of Gideon" (Judg. 6:34). He was a farmer. It can happen to anyone. And it was for the sake of the spirit, *not* for the sake of Gideon.

> And the Lord turned to him and said, "Go in this might of yours and deliver Israel from the hand of Midian; do not I send you?" And he said to him, "Pray, Lord, how can *I* deliver Israel? Behold, my clan is the weakest in Manasseh, and I am the least in my family." And the Lord said to him, "But I will be with you" (Judg. 6:14–16).

We do not possess the spirit, the spirit possesses us. How do we know when we're possessed? When we find ourselves doing something we would not normally do. But that could be the devil, not the spirit. Of course, but keep going. The power of the passive is such that you *will* keep going. Gideon stuck with what was happening to him even though he didn't think he was the one it should be happening to. *Then* he knew. He quit arguing and started experiencing. *Then* he knew. He stopped resisting what was irresistible. *Then* he knew. "You always resist the Holy Spirit," Stephen said to the church people (Acts 7:51). Argumentative, intellectual, refusing to risk the experience, just like us. It was the one thing Jesus could not tolerate. That a person would refuse to be touched by the breath, blown by the wind, struck by the storm. It was the one thing, apparently, that was out of the question for Jesus if a church member was going to live the kind of elemental, unpredictable, irresistible life he or she was capable of living.

> Truly, I say to you, all sins will be forgiven the sons of men, and whatever blasphemies they utter; but whoever blasphemes against the Holy Spirit *never* has forgiveness, but is guilty of an eternal sin (Mark 3:28–29).

The passive was being done before their very eyes, and they were arguing. It was being done to them, and they were resisting. Why? Because they were such activists they had to predict the unpredictable, resist the irresistible, produce the elemental. They would not *be* possessed. Therefore they could never experience the power. The storm would cease. The wind would fade. The breath would die. The opportunity to be a church would be lost.

III

The passive is also the power of the active. Possessed by the spirit, the great passive acts of faith can take place. Faith itself, prayer, healing, preaching—all things we would not normally do but which are now being done through us. Justice. Possessed by the spirit, a passive person is now obsessed by a cause.

> I will put my Spirit upon him.
> and he shall proclaim justice to the Gentiles.
>
> (Matt. 12:18)

> I have put my Spirit upon him,
> he will bring forth justice to the nations.
>
> (Isa. 42:1)

> I am filled with power,
> with the Spirit of the Lord,
> and with justice.
>
> (Mic. 3:8)

None of the prophets chose to prophesy. None of the leaders chose to lead. None of the servants chose to serve. "Behold, my servant whom I have chosen" (Matt. 12:18). That was the point. Not that they had chosen but that they had *been* chosen. Not that they were leading but that they were being led. Justice is done through us not by us. It is not something *we* would normally do.

Amos would have preferred to tend to his business interests. Isaiah would have preferred to stick to his temple interests. Gideon would have preferred to remain on the farm. Moses would have preferred to remain with the sheep. But it was not to be so. They were in the grip of the spirit. First the breath. Then the wind. Then the storm. "National Political Action."[5]

First the possession, then the obsession. What is the cause that uses you? That you live, eat, breathe, sleep, taste? That bothers your appetite? That keeps you awake at night? It is said that the biggest cause for most Americans is How can I take off five pounds and Where can I find a place to park? But what about the justice of a corporation that eliminates its competition? What about the justice of a church that gives away only twenty cents of every dollar? What about the justice, according to Forbes magazine, of the fact that one-half of all American families can afford to spend no more than fifteen thousand dollars for a house and that less than one of every four families can afford the average new house, priced at around twenty-five thousand dollars?[6]

It is immensely instructive that the coming of the spirit in the Bible is related to the coming of justice. It is equally instructive that the coming of the spirit in our time is often totally unrelated to the coming of justice. It is precisely those who feel they have a corner on the spirit who depreciate the need to work for justice. Indeed, the foremost exponent of "conservative" Christianity in America was heard loudly proclaiming on nationwide television September 7, 1971, and I quote: "Stay out of politics and go all the way with Jesus." That is absurd. More to the point: it is biblically illiterate.

We need church people, men and women, young men and young women, possessed by the spirit, who are obsessed by justice. Who will speak for it. Who will work for it. Who will live it, eat it, breathe it, sleep it, die it. Who will *prove* the spirit *by* the justice.

> No prophecy ever came by the impulse of *man*, but men moved by the Holy *Spirit* spoke from *God* (2 Pet. 1:21).
>
> It is not *you* who speak, but the Spirit of your Father speaking *through* you (Matt. 10:20).

If there is no spirit, then there can be no justice. But if there is no justice, then there is no spirit. The storm has ceased. The wind has failed. The breath has gone. The church has died.

IV

Finally, the passive brings the power to change. It is a great power. It is, of course, not the power to change at all, but the power to *be* changed. It is what the spirit is all about, and it has stunned men and women for centuries.

Ezekiel put it well in the valley of dry bones: "O dry bones, hear the word of the Lord. . . . Behold, I will cause breath to enter you, and you shall live" (Ezek. 37:4–5). The spirit is not only elemental in the sense of being the life force. It is also elemental in the sense of being the new-life force. It is not only the capacity to make new but the capacity to renew. And that is what is exciting to people in the grip of the passive. They can be "born anew" (John 3:3).

> Then the spirit of the Lord will come mightily upon you, and you shall prophesy with them and be turned into *another man* (1 Sam. 10:6).

It was unbelievable.

> And when all who knew him before saw how he prophesied with the prophets, the people said to one another, "What has come over the son of Kish? Is Saul also among the prophets?" (1 Sam. 10:11).

It was the power to be changed that dumbfounded the early church members. They called it the "new creation."

> If any one is in Christ, he is a new creation; the old has passed away, behold, the new has come. All this is from *God* (2 Cor. 5:17–18).

It couldn't have been from them. Who can change himself? The fact that they were changed proved God.

> A new heart *I* will give you, and a new spirit *I* will put within you; . . . And *I* will put my spirit within you, . . . and *I* will be your God (Ezek. 36:26, 27, 28).

They couldn't do it. It was beyond them. They *were* changed. Now they had the power to face themselves. The spirit drove Jesus into the wilderness (Matt. 4:1). They had the power to face others. The spirit told them how to speak (Acts 4:31, Matt. 10:

20). They had the power to face Christ. "No one can say 'Jesus is Lord' except by the Holy Spirit" (1 Cor. 12:3). And they had the power to face the ultimate in passivity, their own deaths. Stephen, "full of the Holy Spirit" (Acts 7:55), as they seize him and murder him. Talk about change. How could anyone be more *changed* than that? "Thanks be to God," one of them cried, "for his inexpressible gift!" (2 Cor. 9:15).

The church are the changed people. They are the power-ful people. The in-spir-ed people. The spirit-ed people. The passive people.

They are also the agents of change. They are being used by the spirit. "Sent out by the Holy Spirit" (Acts 13:4). To "turn the world upside down" (Acts 17:6). The power is the *same*. "Clothed with power from on high" (Luke 24:49). If only we would use it. If only we would let ourselves *be* used by it. "I will pour water on the thirsty land" (Isa. 44:3). But we resist. "And streams on the dry ground" (Isa. 44:3). But we resist. "O land, land, land, hear the word of the Lord!" (Jer. 22:29).

First the breath. Then the wind. Then the storm. First the spirit. Then the passive. Then the church.

NOTES

1. S. V. McCasland in *The Interpreter's Dictionary of the Bible* (New York: Abingdon, 1962), vol. 4, p. 432.
2. *Idem.*
3. H. Kleinknecht in G. Friedrich, *Theological Dictionary of the New Testament* (Grand Rapids, Mich.: Eerdmans, 1968), vol. 6, p. 335.
4. G. W. H. Lampe in S. V. McCasland, *op. cit.*, vol. 2, pp. 626–629; S. V. McCasland, *op. cit.*, p. 433; F. Baumgartel in H. Kleinknecht, *op. cit.*, p. 365.
5. F. Baumgartel, *op. cit.*, p. 366.
6. *Forbes Magazine*, 1 January 1971.

13

THE POINT IS TO BE HUMILIATED

I

You begin with the premise that a church member knows what he's doing. It is, of course, a hazardous premise, but, for most, probably an accurate one. We know what we're doing, or we wouldn't be doing it. This does not mean we know why we're doing it. Nor does it mean we know how to do it. But it does mean we know what we're doing. We have chosen to do this and not that. We are that much in control.

Paul had a plan. He would persecute Christians. Moses had a plan. He would look after his father-in-law's business. Isaiah had a plan. He would be a temple priest. Saul had a plan. He would work for his father.

Most of us have some sort of plan for where we're going. We know what we're doing, or we wouldn't be doing it. We have taken this job and not that. We have gone to this school and not that. We have chosen this community service and not that. We have chosen this church and not that.

We're organized. We're in control. We have a plan. We're doing our best to work it. We're trying to maximize ourselves. We're trying to be who we are. We even had a "game plan" for our nation. We tried to maximize it. Anything to stand on our own two feet. Anything to be in control. Anything to be on top. Anything to be the people we are capable of becoming.

II

And none of it is any good. It gets church members nowhere. It is in the wrong direction. It refers to the one who makes more of himself than the reality justifies.[1] Who promises what he cannot perform. Who wants to be high[2] when he should be low. Who wants to be active when he should be passive.

> Though you soar aloft like the eagle,
>   though your nest is set among the stars,
>   thence I will bring you *down,* says the Lord.
>   (Obad. 4)

You can't stand on your own feet. You can't be on top. You can't be in control. You can't maximize yourself. It is not in your power. It is not in your control. The Bible ridicules people who think they are in control of their lives.

> Come now, you who say, "Today or tomorrow we will go into such and such a town and spend a year there and trade and get gain"; whereas you do not *know* about tomorrow. What is your life? For you are a *mist* that appears for a little time and then vanishes. Instead you ought to say, "If the *Lord* wills, we shall live and we shall do this or that" (James 4:13–15).

But we won't say that. It is not in the human condition to say it. We won't say it until we have been brought low. We won't maximize ourselves until we have minimized ourselves. And we won't do that. We can't stand on our own feet, but we don't know that until we have been knocked off our feet. It is too much to ask an active church member to become passive. No wonder people are leaving churches. It is more than the reality justifies. He has to *be* brought low. He has to *be* humiliated. God *is* what brings a person low. "Thence I will bring you down, says the Lord." God *is* what humiliates us.

> Have you entered into the springs of the sea,
>   or walked in the recesses of the deep?
> Have the gates of death been revealed to you,
>   or have you seen the gates of deep darkness?
> Have you comprehended the expanse of the earth?
>   Declare, if you know all this.
>
> (Job 38:16–18)

There are no self-made men in the Bible. All the biblical heroes are passivists. All are men and women who were brought low. Whose plans were interrupted. Who were humiliated. Who were used. Paul, by the side of the road. Moses, terrified at the bush. Isaiah, dumbfounded in the temple. Jeremiah, used. Saul, used. David, used. Jesus, used. Indeed, the point of the wilderness is precisely that Jesus would *be* planned, *be* controlled, *be* humiliated, even to the point of the ultimate humiliation, death on a cross. The incarnation was humiliation.

*

No, the humiliating experiences need not be negative. The birth of a child, as we say, is "a very humbling experience." Or alone in the woods on a snowy evening. Or before a work of art. Or before another who has touched your life. It was the most positive experience Paul ever had. Same for Moses. Same for Isaiah. Same for Jeremiah, Saul, David, Jesus. The point is simply that the humiliating experiences for the church member must come. We *must* be brought low. Our pretensions *must* be ridiculed. *If* we want to fulfill ourselves as churches. Correction: *be* fulfilled.

But isn't that an assumption? That I cannot be who I was meant to be on my own? That I need help? That I particularly need the help of defeat before victory, of humiliation before fulfillment?

Certainly it is an assumption. It is the biblical assumption. We are what God does to us, and we won't be what we can be until God has done it. Try it any other way and see if it works. The only test is pragmatic. If you can be more of a church without being brought low, fine. But you'd better know what you're doing because the weight of historical evidence, according to the Bible, is against you.

> Whom are you like in your greatness?
> Behold, I will liken you to a cedar in Lebanon,
> with fair branches and forest shade,
>> and of great height,
>> its top among the clouds. . . .
>
> Therefore thus says the Lord God: Because it towered high and set its top among the clouds, . . . I have cast it out (Ezek. 31:2–3, 10–11).

III

But doesn't this give a person a low self-image? And isn't the problem with the world, as modern psychology is suggesting, precisely that we have too many people with too low self-images?

Quite to the contrary. The problem is that we have too many church members with too high self-images for which there is no justification. That is why the incarnation was humiliation. And that is why the first Christians called themselves, as we have seen, by the one word that was the essence of humiliation, "slaves."

> Paul, a slave of Jesus Christ (Rom. 1:1).
>
> James, a slave of God and . . . Christ (James 1:1).
>
> Peter, a slave . . . of Jesus Christ (2 Pet. 1:1).
>
> Jude, a slave of . . . Jesus Christ (Jude 1).

It was the only way they could handle it. It was the only way they could insure the victory of the passive over the active. It was the only way they could reach the self-fulfillment through the self-destruction.

*

But is that the kind of church we want? If we want to set out to humiliate everyone, won't that leave us without any church leadership, without any glue?

Not at all. It will give us precisely the glue we have been looking for. Instead of every church madly pursuing its own self-interest we just may have people pursuing each other's interests. "Through love be slaves of one another" (Gal. 5:13). It could be the answer we have been looking for. "In humility count others better than yourselves" (Phil. 2:3). It meant a reasonable deference to the interests of others. Talk about peace. Are not the seeds for peace in being men and women for others? "Be subject to one another out of reverence for Christ" (Eph. 5:21).

Not giants but subjects. Not "pitiful, helpless giants" and not "sleeping giants" either. Not giants but slaves. Even the church is suspect. Especially the church is suspect. If it is princely rather than slavish. If it is gigantic rather than feeble. If it refuses to be humiliated.

> Behold, I will *profane* my sanctuary, the pride of your power, the delight of your eyes, and the desire of your soul (Ezek. 24:21).

> Shall the axe vaunt itself over him who hews with it,
>   or the saw magnify itself against him who wields it?
> As if a rod should wield him who lifts it,
>   or as if a staff should lift him who is not wood!
>   (Isa. 10:15)

*

But doesn't this create a dangerous dependency syndrome? If a church member is going to be a slave, he is going to have to depend on his master. Indeed, he is totally dependent on his master. Indeed, he is *nothing* apart from his master.

Yes, that is the point. It is precisely what the humiliation is expected to do. It is *expected* to create dependency. That is what it is *for*. "It is no longer I who live," Paul said, "but Christ who lives in me" (Gal. 2:20). Indeed, as we have seen, he carried it so far as to admit, "I am nothing" (2 Cor. 12:11). Total dependence was the *ideal*. Not the syndrome but the cure. Not the one thing to be avoided but the one thing to be sought. "If any man would come after me, let him *deny* himself. . . . Whoever *loses* his life for my sake will find it" (Matt. 16:24–25).

When were you last brought down? What knocked your feet out from under you? That *was* God in your life. No, that is not all God is, but God is at least that. It was an attempt to reverse the direction of your life. It was an attempt to bring you off the height into the depth, off the mountain into the valley. It was an attempt to find *you*, to fulfill *you*, to create in you precisely the dependency you needed in order to be *you*.

*

But doesn't the church member have *something* to do with it? After all I am a person. I am a human being, and human beings do act. They do have *some* control.

No, the Bible won't even give you that. "Not that we are sufficient of ourselves to claim *anything* as coming from us" (2 Cor. 3:5). "Neither he who plants nor he who waters is *anything*" (1 Cor. 3:7).

But what's that going to do to my self-confidence? Hopefully everything. Hopefully it will *shatter* your self-confidence. Hopefully your self-confidence will be so *broken* that your *only* confidence will be in God. God *is* what picks up the pieces after your humiliation as a church member. "By the grace of *God* I am what I am, . . . it was *not* I, but the grace of *God* which is with me" (1 Cor. 15:10). "It was not because you were more in number than any other people that the Lord set his love upon you and chose you, for you were the fewest of all peoples; but *it is because the Lord loves you*" (Deut. 7:7–8). *You* didn't do it. *You* didn't deserve it. You had *nothing* to do with it. It had to be done *to* you before it could be done *through* you. God *was* what broke you. God *was* what healed you.

*

But that's not my style. I don't run my business that way. I don't run my family that way. And I certainly don't run my church that way.

Forget your style. Nobody cares about your style. This is the passive not the active. These are the things done through us not by us. "I will not . . . speak of *anything* except what Christ has wrought *through* me" (Rom. 15:18). That's the only style that matters now.

Sure it's not easy. Sure it's a wrench. Sure we can't believe it's us. That's the *point.* It *isn't* us. We have been humiliated to the point where *we* don't do it. If *we* were doing it, it would never be done because it would never get in our life plan or church plan in the first place. "The sacrifice acceptable to God is a broken spirit" (Ps. 51:17). But we are not about to break our spirits. We have to *be* broken in order that we can *be* ridden. *Then* the power courses.

Paul was beaten. Moses was scared. Isaiah ignored. Jeremiah jailed. Saul opposed. David bereaved. Jesus killed. There is no way to avoid the agony of the wrench in your style, but it must be kept in perspective. Remember, the experience is ultimately positive no matter how proximately negative. That is why Paul can, as he says, boast of his sufferings (2 Cor. 11:21, 12:9). Not of his achievements. That would be active. But of his sufferings. They *prove* God. "We have this treasure in earthen vessels, to show that the transcendent power belongs to *God* and not to us" (2 Cor. 4:7). God is using the vessel. He humiliates it, then he uses it. And in the using, it is more and more abused. But that does not matter. "My grace is sufficient for you, for my *power* is made perfect in *weakness*" (2 Cor. 12:9). The weakness of the slave *proves* the power of the master.

Ah, but if that's the price I have to pay, I don't want that kind of power. You don't? Think for a moment. It is the greatest power in the history of the world. "He was crucified in weakness, but lives by the power of God" (2 Cor. 13:4). Nothing has ever been able to touch it. Nothing will ever be able to touch it for *us*, and we had better think about that because our humiliation as church members *will* come. We *will* be broken. "Every one who exalts himself *will* be humbled" (Luke 14:11), the crucified man said. We *will* be brought low.

And that is as it should be. Humiliation is the point, not growth. And we will not be without resource. The power of the passive will sustain us. "I can do *all* things in him who strengthens me" (Phil. 4:13). "When I am weak, *then* I am strong" (2 Cor. 12:10). Only the mastered can master. Only the slave can be free. Only the weak can know power. Only the humbled can rule.

> Give glory to the Lord your God
>   before he brings darkness,
> before your feet stumble
>   on the twilight mountains,
> and while you look for light
>   he turns it into gloom
>   and makes it deep darkness.
> But if you will not listen,
>   my soul will weep in secret for your pride.
>   (Jer. 13:16–17)

NOTES

1. G. Delling in G. Kittel, *Theological Dictionary of the New Testament* (Kalamazoo, Mich.: Eerdmans, 1964), vol. 1, p. 226.
2. The Hebrew for "pride" comes from the root for "to be high." J. A. Wharton in *The Interpreter's Dictionary of the Bible* (New York: Abingdon, 1962), vol. 3, p. 876.

14

THE POINT IS DISCLOSURE

I

What is the point of church membership? After all is said and done, What is it I get from church that I don't get anywhere else? What is it I do in church that I don't do anywhere else? Why should church membership be an option in my life? Particularly when I am in college. Particularly when I have the mortgage to pay.

It is obvious that I live in the dimension of self. We call this dimension psychology. It is obvious that I live in the dimension of others. We call it sociology. It is obvious that I live in the dimension of nature, environment, world. We call the dimension ecology. But it is not at all obvious that I live in a fourth dimension, the dimension of theology, the dimension we call God, which is presumably mediated by the church.

How does the church member *know* there is a fourth dimension? We have read about it. We have heard about it. Perhaps it has even been described to us personally, but that does not mean we have experienced it. It does not mean we really *know* anything about it.

It is one thing to know about self. We are involved. We cannot get out of the dimension. We live it, eat it, breathe it, sleep it. Our problem is the opposite of the fourth dimension. The first we cannot get out of. The fourth we cannot get into. The first we cannot objectify. The fourth cannot objectify us.

112

It is the same with the second. We are all involved with other people. They are unavoidable, and that is all right. They are desirable. But the fourth dimension, though desirable, perhaps, is avoidable. I can live every day of the week in singular detachment from God. I cannot do so from other people. Again, my problem is to get out of the second dimension and into the fourth.

What about the third? I cannot go out of my house without being involved in the world about me. I cannot stay in my house without being involved. But the fourth dimension—there is nothing pressuring me to go into it. I do not go out of my house and bump into God the way I can go out of my house and bump into a tree.

Why should I? More to the point, why should I want to? Granted that I have heard, read, even had the fourth dimension described. Why should I want to go into it? There is nothing in the descriptions that is compelling. I heard one on vacation once that was—to put it charitably—not exciting. I heard one on another Sunday that was a waste of time. If even the professionals who are supposed to make their living cajoling people into the fourth dimension are so devoid of imagination as to be unable to dredge me out of my three, what hope is there that I will ever encounter the fourth?

And even granted that the descriptions exist. Even granted that some are more compelling than others. Granted even that there is one poet somewhere who can intrigue me with the fourth dimension, that does not prove that the fourth dimension *exists*. That does not prove that I am *in* it. Or that I think I am in it. Or that it is real to me but not to anyone else. I want that fourth dimension to be there as much as the tree in my front yard. I want to be able to run into it. I want to be able to live it, eat it, breathe it, sleep it, too.

Why? *Why* does a person want the fourth dimension? Why does he want the hearsay when he can have the straight story? Why does he want the fourth when he can have the three? Indeed, why does he want the fourth when, if he gets it, he is in danger of *losing* the three? Isn't that what happens to people who get so turned on by God they turn off other people? Don't I have to leave other people *behind* if I go for the fourth? Don't I have to leave myself *behind?* The world? "If any one would come after me, he must leave self behind." A man of the fourth dimension *said* that.

But I don't *want* to leave anything behind. The fourth dimension is *not* that desirable. That's a price *I* don't want to pay. Therefore I will give it a once-a-week shot but no more. Not at that price. Yes, the once-a-week may not be enough to experience it. Yes, it may not be enough to give it a fair chance. Yes, the once-a-week is often a waste of even that much time. But no, I am not willing to pay the price of the fourth dimension if it means leaving the other three behind. What am I, a hermit? An ascetic?

Then why don't you take it all with you? Fine, but I thought you just said you had to leave it all behind. Perhaps. For some people. Maybe this *is* the way *they* have to go into the fourth dimension. But what about *you?* How do you have to go?

I wish I knew. If only you could know how it had to be for you. But no, I will not even go that far. We have the cart before the horse. It has not been demonstrated *why* I should go, let alone how. I want to know *why. Why* is the fourth dimension so desirable? Particularly, why is it desirable if, as seems inevitable, any time in the fourth will take me away from the three? And life is too short, isn't it, to be stealing time from the three dimensions which are there like trees for the sake of a fourth which is there like a mirage?

There is only one answer. Life is too short, isn't it, to be lived at only 75 percent? Beyond that, what can be said? That the church member will be better? Not necessarily. The Inquisition gave a lot of time to the fourth dimension. That the church member will be happier? Not necessarily. Jeremiah was unhappy. So was Jesus. He even wept. That the church member will think positively? Not necessarily. I may think very negatively about some things, like economic and social injustice, the way Amos did, and Isaiah. No, all that can be said is that I will have made a stab at living in four dimensions out of four. And that when I die I will be able to say that at least I tried to live a full life. I could not live in only three dimensions when I had heard, read, even been bored by the possibility of a fourth.

II

How, then, to go into it? *First,* the church member does everything in his power. He pulls out all the stops. And if a person is living deeply in the first three dimensions, he will have a lot of stops to pull. We read. We sing. We worship. We go into all the arts. We meditate. We pray. We reflect. We scour history. We may even go into ESP, spiritual healing, hypnosis, Yoga, psychic phenomena. Why not? " 'When you seek me with all your heart, I will be found by you,' says the Lord" (Jer. 29:13–14).

Only, of course, it doesn't happen that easily. Church members try, but they don't succeed. We get only so far, and it isn't really very far. Soon we fall victim to our inveterate tendency to reduce the complex to the simple, to remove the mystery from the mysterious, to think we have someone or something, and now God, when we haven't. As we have seen, the word the ancient Jews had for "holy" meant "separate."[1] The idea was that God was God and man was man. God *was* what man could not get at, could not pollute, could not win a war against, could not control. "Our God is holy!" (Ps. 99:9). It meant God *was* what could *not* be reduced: the quark behind the quark, the self behind the other, the you behind the you. God *is* the intelligence behind the universe, the love behind the relationship, the mystery behind the self.

Only we demystify all that. We go charging out of the three dimensions to attack the fourth, and what do we find? We find that it won't yield. So what do we do? We attack all the harder. We read the Bible on Sundays. We pray in the morning as well as the evening. We buy books on Edgar Cayce. We write sermons and talk in our small groups until midnight.

What is it that we are trying to do? We are trying to wrest the meaning out of the mystery, just as we tried to wrest the secret out of the atom and out of the self and out of the other. And that is legitimate. Make no mistake. It is legitimate because it is us, it is human. But it does *not* get us into the fourth dimension. It may get us on our *way.* It may be a first step. But it does not get us *there.*

Why? Because in trying to demystify the mysterious, church members have profaned the holy. We have tried to make it ours when we are its. We have treated it as an object when it was the subject. We have been presumptuous enough to think we could handle it, forgetting that to touch the holy mountain was to die (Exod. 19:12). We have tried, in other words, to do in the fourth dimension what we have already done in the other three. When you take the holy out of a person, you can kill him. When you take the holy out of nature, you can ravage it. When you take the holy out of yourself, you can give up.

III

But this time it won't work. If we are going to make it into the fourth dimension, we must do the *opposite* of presume. We must wrench our styles. We must *be* wrenched. We must bow before the holy, not storm it. We must submit, not assault. We must, of all things, relax, not aggress. "Be still, and know that I am God" (Ps. 46:10). The holy is *what we can't get at,* but we don't *know* that until we have been repulsed. No, not always, but often. A church *plans* its assaults to *be* assaulted. *Then* we kneel—*if* we will. It is the *second* step, but it does not *have* to be taken. When I know that I cannot reach the holy on my own, I can either keep my style and despair, or change my style and kneel. The despair is a live option. It accounts for plenty of people leaving the church.

> One can imagine this vulnerable, quiet man [James Dickey writes of the poet Edwin Arlington Robinson] . . . sitting in a chair staring at his own nondescript image in the mirror, his eyes fiery with unwitnessed crying, his knuckles at his lips, asking questions about himself, about other people, and getting nothing back. It is harrowing. Most of us think now and then, that there aren't any answers, but Robinson *knows* there aren't.[2]

God reveals *himself.* It is the ultimate affront. A man is minding his own business, Moses, and God is there. A teenager is minding his, Jeremiah, and God is there. David, Saul, Samuel, Gideon, Solomon, Peter, Paul, all of them, surprised by God. "The Old Testament," writes an expert, "does *not* purport to be the record of human initiative in seeking for and discovering God, for—as the author of Job realized—God would elude men's search *completely* unless God *on his own initiative* were to reveal himself and speak his word."[3]

Let it be. Leave the fourth dimension alone, and it will happen. Stop trying. That doesn't mean not to try. It means you have to know when to *stop* trying. Lean back. Relax. God is what you *can't* get at. Back off. He is what you can't equate, can't paint, can't sing, can't buy, can't write. Revelation is *precisely* what you do *not* discover but what discovers *you.* But you do not *know* that, you do not discover it, until you have done everything in your power *to* discover it. *Then* it comes—maybe. *Then* you kneel—maybe. *Then* you rest—maybe. *Then* you are afraid. "It is a fearful thing to fall into the hands of the living God" (Heb. 10:31). Then you *are* discovered.

No one's style is changed that much without being afraid. Fear is what happens when, as we say, we get out of our depth, when we go into a new situation, a new group, a new environment. And fear is the emotion felt by the ancient people of the fourth dimension when they *knew* they were in it. Isaiah was afraid when he was called (Isa. 6:5). Jacob was afraid (Gen. 28:17). Moses afraid

(Exod. 3:6). Why not? They were men. They lived in the three dimensions, and now the fourth was coming at them. They knew it was there because they were terrified. Have you ever been scared by your church?

No, that is not the only way the fourth dimension comes. But it is one way, and it is a way that modern man, with all his discoveries in the first three, has lost. Proof of the loss of the holy is our loss of fear. "Is the Lord among us or not?" (Exod. 17:7).

> The Lord your God is a devouring fire (Deut. 4:24).
>
> The Lord of hosts, him you shall regard as holy; let him be your *fear*, and let him be your *dread* (Isa. 8:13).
>
> Serve the Lord with *fear*, with trembling kiss his feet (Ps. 2:11–12).
>
> I will give them one heart and one way, that they may *fear* me for ever (Jer. 32:39).

The holy brought fear. You knew you were in touch with God when you were afraid. You were afraid because you were out of control. Something was controlling *you*. "*All* the traditions of the self-disclosure of God . . . suggest in one way or . . . another [that] . . . there is a mystery in divine holiness which produces in man a sense of terror."[4]

Jesus, afraid in the garden. Jesus, afraid on the cross. "Work out your own salvation," Paul wrote, "with *fear* and trembling" (Phil. 2:12). "It is . . . a grave error to maintain, with many moderns, that Christianity, as opposed to Hebraism, has replaced the fear of God by the love of God."[5]

It is also a grave error to assume that fear is merely negative. Far from it. "The fear of the Lord, that is *wisdom*," a man wrote (Job 28:28). "His *mercy* is on those who fear him," Mary sings (Luke 1:50). "This fear is not the result of God's destroying wrath or condemning judgment. It arises from the perception of his very love, unmerited, gratuitous, unearned."[6] Indeed, the "fear

of the Lord" was the phrase used to express complete *faith*.[7]
Holiness meant *love*.[8]

Just as church members feel they are personally incomplete
without the fourth dimension, so they feel they are emotionally
incomplete without fear. That may not lead to church growth, but
that is not the point. Fear is the emotion of the fourth dimension.
Not the only emotion, but one emotion, and an important one.
Why? Because it lets the mysterious be mysterious. It lets the holy
be holy. It helps a partial person be whole.

So what are we left with? That the fourth dimension is possible? Yes. That it is desirable? Perhaps. That it is necessary? If you
want a full life. That it is inevitable? By no means. That it is
fearful? Yes. "It is a fearful thing to fall into the hands of the
living God." And that out of the fear comes joy? Yes. "Fear seized
them all," it is reported of Jesus, "and they glorified God, saying,
'A great prophet has arisen among us!' and 'God has visited his
people!' " (Luke 7:16)

NOTES

1. James Muilenburg in *The Interpreter's Dictionary of the Bible* (New York:
      Abingdon, 1962), vol. 2, p. 617.
2. James Dickey in *The New York Times Book Review*, 18 May 1969 (ital. his).
3. B. W. Anderson in Muilenburg, *op. cit.*, p. 419 (ital. add.).
4. Samuel Terrien in Muilenburg, *op. cit.*, p. 257 (ital. add.).
5. *Ibid.*, p. 259.
6. *Ibid.*, p. 258.
7. *Ibid.*, p. 259.
8. Muilenburg, *op. cit.*, p. 622.

15

THE POINT IS PEACE

It could be argued that there is nothing churches can do. Of the 3,469 years of recorded history, according to the military analyst of the New York *Times,* only 227 have known peace.[1] A statistic like that does not augur well for peace.

By the same token it could be argued that churches can do quite a lot. There are even those who advocate the convention of a world constitutional assembly and who say that once we have the constitution the peace will follow.

In either event, we are perhaps best served by turning to what many would argue is the world's best source book on human nature, which is where wars begin and end. The Bible has its cynics and it has its utopians. It has its realists and its idealists.

I

First, the Bible speaks of peace within. It is what we might call psychological peace. The word for peace in the Hebrew, *shalom,* comes from the root for completeness, wholeness.[2] An integrated personality, we say, is "at peace." And in the Bible there are numerous examples of people who are "at peace," as we say, "with themselves." Look at David, Moses, Peter, Paul, Jesus, Ruth. In spite of their struggles, they exemplified peace.

This peace within was sufficiently strong to be accompanied by peace without. That is to say, psychological peace was often accompanied by economic and even medical well-being. People who had *shalom* were people who were well off and well.[3] Peace brings prosperity (Ps. 37:37). It brings length of life (Prov. 3:2). It brings a peaceful death (Gen. 15:15). It even brings, as we have all experienced, sleep (Ps. 4:8).

Perhaps *serenity* would be the best word to describe inner peace. We all know people whom we would call serene. They are whole people. They are complete. They are integrated. There are one or two such people in everyone's life. Often they are in good circumstances. If they are not, it doesn't matter. They are that serene. Often they are in good health. If they are not, it doesn't matter. Their peace within is such that they can handle anything.

Surely one point of religion is peace within. No religion would last if it didn't bring that peace. It was "distinctively Christian," an expert writes.[4] "Peace I leave with you," Jesus said, "my peace I give to you" (John 14:27). "To set the mind on the Spirit," Paul wrote, "is life and peace" (Rom 8:6). "The fruit of the Spirit," he said, "is love, joy, peace" (Gal. 5:22). "Let the peace of Christ rule in your hearts" (Col. 3:15).

II

But there was more to peace than that. The word had other dimensions. We get into a great deal of trouble if we stop at peace within. That's safe. Everybody wants peace within. It's safe to belong to a church that deals only with peace within— with yourself and your hang-ups and your wars. But that is precisely one reason the church is no longer cutting it with a great many people. It has preferred the safety of peace within to the risk of peace between. It has preferred the safety of psychological peace to the risk of sociological peace. It has preferred the safety of one part of the gospel to the risk of the whole gospel.

Indeed, we have it reversed. The psychological is the *by-product* of the sociological in the Bible. Peace between comes *before* peace within. It is not a matter of my getting peace within and then going out and spreading peace between. It is a matter of going out and spreading peace between and *then* maybe yes maybe *not* getting peace within.

David at peace? When he was being attacked by his own son? Moses at peace? When they fought him every inch of the way? "What shall I do with this people?" (Exod. 17:4). Peter at peace when he denies Jesus? Paul at peace when they reject him in Athens? Jesus at peace when he is in agony in Gethsemane? Ruth at peace as a foreigner?

Their peace came last not first. The important thing was what you were doing for peace between, not how you felt about peace within. You might be feeling very badly, but that didn't matter. Or, if it mattered, it mattered second, not first. You came second, others came first.

> If you are offering your gift at the altar [Jesus said] and there remember that your brother has something against you, leave your gift there before the altar and go; *first* be reconciled to your brother, and then come and offer your gift (Matt. 5:23–24).

This is not to say that peace within is not important. Of course it's important. But it's last, not first. And it may not even be at all. "My God, my God, why hast thou forsaken me?" (Matt. 27: 46). Do you call that peace? The modern church has it backwards and has had it backwards for twenty-five years. We have everyone pursuing "peace of mind" when we should have everyone pursuing the peace of the world, from which pursuit you may or may not get peace of mind. "If any man would come after me, let him deny himself and take up his cross" (Mark 8:34). The cross is the

Christian symbol, not the cross-legged contemplative. Self-giving is the formula for peace, not self-fulfillment. Self-giving is the Christian ideal, not self-fulfillment. Peace between is the goal, from which you may or may not get peace within. Indeed, it is so thoroughly absorbed into the Judeo-Christian tradition that an astounded expert can write: "When we consider the rich possibilities of *shalom* in the Old Testament, we are struck by the . . . fact that there is *no* specific text in which it denotes the specifically spiritual attitude of inward peace."[5] Invariably it refers to the group. And invariably it refers to what that group is doing for justice, righteousness, peace. "In its most common use *shalom* is an emphatically *social* concept."[6] A church, then, is measured, *not* by what it does for peace within, but by what it does for peace between, from which its members may or may not get peace within. And that is hard for many church members to take.

III

All right. That is all well and good, but *how* does a church give itself? If the cause of peace is to be served by those who give themselves, *how* do people give themselves? They don't. They won't. They can't. It is beyond them. It is something *they* can't do. They would rather be contemplative than crucified. We would rather fulfill ourselves than give ourselves.

We have to keep moving in our quest for peace. More to the point, we have to get the order of our movement straight. Peace within, which appears to be first, is *last.* Peace between is *second.* Peace beyond is *first.* We have to go beyond ourselves if we are ever going to have peace. Left to our devices we cannot do it. The League of Nations was not enough. The United Nations is not enough. Our inveterate nationalisms are not enough.

It goes to the root of human nature. It is just too much to ask a church—let alone a country—to give itself. It goes against our grain. More accurately, it presents such a threat to our psychological peace that we won't do it. That is why churches have to be the done-to. Active people have to become passive. It is the *only* way we can go beyond our inability to give ourselves and *find* ourselves giving ourselves. God *is* what we find ourselves doing for peace.

All right, *how* are we done to? How do we become passive? It's happening *all the time.* Every day, virtually every hour, there are challenges for self-giving. *We* did not put those challenges there. They *are* there. They come at us all the time. They *are* the grace of God. Insofar as you accept the challenge and give yourself, that is your faith. The action is the response, not the belief. You don't know anything about what you believe, only about what you do. Grace is being done to. Faith is letting it be done. Works is being done through. The old dichotomy couldn't be less helpful. What you do *is* what you believe. If you don't do it, then you don't believe it.

"What do we have to believe to join the church?" a ninth-grader asked. "You don't have to believe anything," is the only reply. But you have to *do* everything. And *you* aren't going to do it. It has to be done to you, then through you. Then you will look back in astonishment on all your self-giving, and that will be what you believe.

*

But individual self-giving is not enough for peace. It is one of the great cop-outs to say I will work for peace on everything that comes my way and then limit everything that comes my way to having a small circle of friends, going to work and back, up to the lake for the weekend, and so on.

The church is the place where people learn how to give themselves. More accurately the church *are* the people who give themselves. Then when you are hurt and your psychological peace is destroyed, the church *are* the people who surround you with their peace between, and you are kept close by the peace beyond. But it is that peace beyond which continues to drive you collectively if you are a church. You begin to respond to challenges that were there *all along*, which alone you had not seen but which together now you do see. Theological peace has opened up sociological, just the way sociological opened up psychological. All three were included in the word *shalom.*[7]

If, for instance, it is true that there can be no peace without self-giving; and if it is true that there can be no self-giving apart from a power beyond us to get us to give ourselves; and if we find that power most dynamically exemplified in a man on a cross; if, in other words, we find *acts of self-giving being done through us because of Jesus,* then I should imagine our enthusiasm for him, the Prince of Peace, would be such that we would do, of all things, one thing open to Christians to do and to do on a large scale. Not just writing our congressmen, important as that is. Not just supporting the UN, important as that is. Not only supporting Members of Congress for Peace through Law, important as that is. But supporting the Christian enterprise sufficiently so that the peaceful news of the self-giving of the cross can be carried around the world.

The sad fact of the matter is that Christian missionaries have had to be brought back from all over the world because there just is not enough money to send them out. The sad fact of the matter is that the average Protestant is so stunned by the self-giving of the cross that he gives the equivalent of a pack of Life Savers a *week* to getting the peaceful news around the world.

Jesus is the way to peace. "He *is* our peace;" exclaimed a first-century Christian (Eph. 2:14). That was the Good News. That the peace beyond had invaded the peace between and made possible the peace within. Yes, the same had been done through the prophets and the Hebrew people. Yes, it had been done through Buddha. Yes, it has been done through people of goodwill everywhere. But it was uniquely done through Jesus. Don't ask how. Simply tell of a cross and watch the dynamic work. And then tell of more than a cross. Tell how the peace beyond was so active and the man so passive that even death itself was beaten. And watch the dynamic work.

"*He* is our peace." No, you cannot explain it. All you can do is tell a story, your story. About how it was for you, a church member, when you last gave yourself, and how you would not have done it if it hadn't been for him. That is all you can say, but it is powerful, very powerful. Because through you, and through an extension of yourself when you cannot go, the story is being told of how peace between is possible because peace beyond is powerful. *You* didn't have anything to do with it. "While we were yet helpless, . . . Christ died for [us]" (Rom. 5:6). It is being done through you. It is being done in spite of you. That is how powerful it is.

But there is more. You not only tell the story and enable it to be told. You *do* the story—and with far more than your usual run of friends. With them, yes; but with more than them, too. You are humble. It is unbelievable. But is happening. He "emptied himself, taking the form of a slave" (Phil. 2:7). It can't be you because you are not humble, but you *find* yourself humble. You *find* yourself *giving* yourself that much.

First at your church. First *with* your church. Your church *are* the humbled people. That is where you *are* humiliated. The passive is that powerful. We are that powerless, that "helpless," Paul said. What does your church do in your community that shows it is being humbled? That shows it is being used? That gives itself in love to the uttermost, so much that its members leave it in droves?

NOTES

1. Hanson W. Baldwin, quoted by Russell Baker, *New York Times*, 21 July 1962, (3,457).

2. E. M. Good in *The Interpreter's Dictionary of the Bible* (New York: Abingdon, 1962), vol. 3, p. 705.

3. *Idem.;* W. Foerster in G. Kittel, *Theological Dictionary of the New Testament* (Ann Arbor, Mich.: Eerdmans, 1964), vol. 2, p. 402.

4. C. L. Mitton in Good, *op. cit.,* p. 706.

5. Foerster, *op. cit.,* p. 406 (ital. add.).

6. *Idem.*

7. C. L. Mitton, *loc. cit.*

16

THE POINT IS TO SUFFER

There is, of course, a great deal of suffering in the world. Some of it is ours, some not. We suffer with those who suffer, and when the time comes to do our own suffering, in one way or another we do it.

It was no different, of course, in the first century. The word for suffering came from the word for pressure. There was pressure then as there is now. There was the pressure of want, the pressure of need, the pressure of anxiety, of persecution, of sorrow, of loneliness.

I

One of the first church members suffered. There are a great many other things you can say about him. He taught. He preached. He changed the direction of the world. But one we often lose sight of is that Paul suffered. It was an epitome of the passive. You don't seek suffering. You *are* hurt.

> Five times I have *received* . . . the forty lashes less one. Three times I have *been* beaten with rods; once I *was* stoned. Three times I have *been* shipwrecked; . . . in danger from rivers, danger from robbers, danger from my own people, danger

from Gentiles, danger in the city, danger in the wilderness, danger at sea, danger from false brethren; in toil and hardship, through many a sleepless night, in hunger and thirst, often without food, in cold and exposure (2 Cor. 11:24–27).

As if that were not enough, Paul was given "a thorn in the flesh" (2 Cor. 12:7) to harass him. The best guess is malaria. He had to be rescued from a mob in Jerusalem (Acts 21:27). He fought with the wild animals at Ephesus (1 Cor. 15:32). He lost his job. He lost his home. He lost his family. He lost his country. He lost his religion.

> I have suffered the loss of all things (Phil. 3:8).
>
> I am in peril every hour (1 Cor. 15:30).
>
> I wrote you out of much afflication and anguish of heart and with many tears (2 Cor. 2:4).
>
> We were so utterly, unbearably crushed that we despaired of life itself. . . . We felt that we had received the sentence of death (2 Cor. 1:8–9).
>
> We hunger and thirst, we are ill-clad and buffeted and homeless. . . . We have become, . . . as the refuse of the world, the offscouring of all things (1 Cor. 4:11, 13).

II

Paul endured. It is one thing to suffer; it is another to endure the suffering. Paul was able to endure for the following reasons.

One, he knew it was necessary. Not just inevitable, but necessary. Everyone knows his suffering is inevitable. Not everyone knows it is necessary. Paul did. "The Holy Spirit testifies to me in every city that imprisonment and afflictions await me" (Acts 20:23). That was the inevitability of suffering. Paul was a realist. "I will show him how much he must suffer for the sake of my name" (Acts 9:16). That was the necessity of suffering. Paul was a Christian.

To be a church member *is* to suffer. You cannot be a church member *without* suffering. The cross is a symbol of suffering. It is the church member's symbol. "Persecution," Jesus said, "arises on *account* of the word" (Mark 4:17). "Through many tribulations," Paul said, "we must enter the kingdom of God" (Acts 14:22). "You . . . know," he wrote, "that this is to be our lot" (1 Thess. 3:3). "You received the word," he said, "in much affliction" (1 Thess. 1:6). We are "fellow heirs with Christ," he wrote, "*provided* we suffer with him" (Rom. 8:17). None of that is particularly conducive to church growth.

*

Two, Paul knew, therefore, that his suffering was voluntary as well as involuntary. He chose it. To be a church member *is* to choose suffering. That is not all it means to be a church member, of course, but to be a church member means at least that. Jesus chose to suffer. That was the point of his agony in Gethsemane. He chose the cross. "If any man would come after me, let him . . . take up his cross."

Stephen chose suffering. Paul chose suffering. The disciples chose suffering. The martyrs chose suffering. That is the *point* of church membership. To push ourselves hard to be a church. To show so much love that if necessary (and it is) we suffer. "I will show him how much he must suffer for the sake of my name."

No, it is not masochistic. It is realistic. It is what is *expected* of churches. A church member is one who loves to the point where he suffers. Of course that kind of love is going to hurt. Of course it is going to be persecuted. Of course it is going to be derided. "*Blessed* are you when men revile you and persecute you and utter all kinds of evil against you falsely on my account" (Matt. 5:11).

But how much suffering really is it for churches? "I fought with beasts at Ephesus." "I am in peril every hour." "I have lost everything." Not much when compared with the suffering of the first church.

*

Three, Paul endured his suffering not only because he knew it was necessary. Not only because he knew it was voluntary. But because he knew it was disciplinary. It was a test of his mettle. It was a test of his church membership.

The word that he used is the word for test. It is translated character (Rom. 5:4). It was used of metal that had been passed through fire. It meant tested by fire. A person has character when he has been tested by suffering and endured. "We are afflicted in every way, but not crushed; perplexed, but not driven to despair; persecuted, but not forsaken; struck down, but not destroyed" (2 Cor. 4:8–9). That's character.

The important thing is that without the discipline of suffering there is going to be little character as church members. There is going to be little growth as churches. There is going to be little self-actualization. Just as suffering is necessary if a person is going to be a Christian, so it is disciplinary if a person is going to be human. The word for character also meant valuable, genuine. When a metal was passed through fire and endured, it came out valuable, genuine. A church member has much greater value as a member and he is more genuine as a person when he or she has been tested by suffering and endured. "Blessed is the man who endures trial, for when he has stood the *test* he will receive the crown of life" (James 1:12).

The first church members were imprisoned. They were beaten. They were exiled. They were stoned. They were mobbed. They were murdered. These "people," wrote a contemporary historian, "whom the masses called Christians, . . . were hated for their vicious crimes."[1] To a man, to a woman, to a child, they had character.

III

Paul suffered. He endured. Most important, he prevailed. All suffer. Some endure. Church members prevail. How did he do it?

First, he related his sufferings to the sufferings of Jesus. It may have been presumptuous, but nevertheless he did it. And he had a reason. He viewed Jesus as the prototypical sufferer, the suffering servant. That is why you find a cross in every room in Catholic hospitals.

> That I may . . . share his sufferings (Phil. 3:10).
>
> In my flesh I complete what is lacking in Christ's afflictions (Col. 1:24).
>
> We share abundantly in Christ's sufferings (2 Cor. 1:5).
>
> Rejoice [Peter wrote] in so far as you share Christ's sufferings (1 Pet. 4:13).
>
> These [the Revelation writer wrote of the martyrs] are they who have come out of the great persecution; they have washed their robes and made them white in the blood of the Lamb (Rev. 7:14).

"For the Christian," writes a scholar, "suffering is participation in the sufferings of Christ."[2] To be a church member *is* to suffer because Christ suffered. It is the Christian way. It is the Christian style. The non-Christian derides it, but he feels it. He reviles it, but he believes it. It binds Christian and non-Christian alike to Christ.

My friend[3] was dying in a death camp in Burma in the Second World War. Suddenly at night there appeared a form at his bedside. The other man bound up his wounds and held my friend's head and nursed him back to health. Within two weeks he had left the death house. "Why did you come," my friend asked, "at such risk to yourself?" "Because of Jesus," was the reply. And he told my friend all about Jesus. And word of it spread through the camp. And the camp was transformed. They started a jungle university. And a jungle orchestra. And a jungle lending library with the one Bible on lean for twenty minutes. And then the captors took the Christian who had come to my friend and crucified him. "You became imitators of . . . the Lord, for you received the word in much affliction, . . . so that you became an example to all the believers in Macedonia and Achaia" (1 Thess. 1:6–7).

*

Second, Paul prevailed because he let his suffering do to him what he understood Jesus let *his* suffering do to *him.* He let it humiliate him. He let it reduce him. He let it destroy him. "I am nothing," he said (2 Cor. 12:11). It is the quintessential statement for church members.

Jesus, Paul wrote, "emptied himself [became nothing], taking the form of a slave [a nothing], . . . and . . . humbled himself and became obedient unto death, even death on a cross" (Phil. 2: 7–8). The church member uses his suffering to knock out his props. That is why great strides are made in hospitals. I remember being with a man in a hospital and how he spoke movingly of his experience, of how it had reduced him, stripped him of his props, humbled him. It was the Pauline factor at work. And now that man is making the most extraordinary progress in being a man, in being human, in being himself. I never cease to be amazed at some new thing he has done for his church, for his friends, for justice, for peace.

It is unbelievable the power in humility, the everything in nothing, the new life in death. "When I am weak," Paul said, "then I am strong" (2 Cor. 12:10). Precisely. "If any one is in Christ, he is a new creation" (2 Cor. 5:17). Precisely. When I am nothing, then I am something. Then at last I am on my way to being the person I was meant to be. It sounds crazy, but there it is. "I am speaking as a fool," he said (2 Cor. 11:21). "I am talking like a madman" (2 Cor. 11:23). Few want to talk like that.

*

Third, that is how his suffering gave him God. It "was to make us rely not on ourselves," he wrote, "but on God" (2 Cor. 1:9). That was the point of suffering. Jesus became "obedient unto death." That was the *point* of the cross. "He learned obedience," another Christian put it, "through what he suffered" (Heb. 5:8). That was the *point* of Gethsemane. It was the *point* of the wilderness. To become nothing in order that God could become everything. "He *emptied* himself, taking the form of a *slave.*"

Suffering is a test of whether a church will empty itself and get God or Prometheanize itself and be God. Indeed, the biblical writers were so certain of the possibility of God in these tests that they went so far as to say that the tests themselves *were* God. "*God* tested Abraham," we read in Genesis (22:1), to see if he would be obedient. To see if he would allow himself to be reduced. To see if he would, in the fire laid for his own son, allow himself to be humiliated.

"*God* has come to test you," we read in Exodus (20:20). The Jews read their history as a series of sufferings in which they were being tested by God to see if they would maximize their potential as humans and include God, or minimize their potential and exclude him. "You shall remember all the way which the Lord your God has led you these forty years in the wilderness, that he might *humble* you, *testing* you to know what was in your heart" (Deut. 8:2).[4]

God tested Job. "Behold," he said to the anti-God, "he is in your power" (Job 2:6). And for forty-one chapters Job fights God. He will not submit. He will not be reduced. He will not be humiliated. But he is. *Then* he becomes a man. "I despise myself" (Job

42:6), Job said. "I am nothing," Paul said. "Not my will," said Jesus, "but thine, be done" (Luke 22:42). They all passed the test. God *was* what tested them. God *was* what made them who they were meant to be.

*

Fourth, churches not only endure, they prevail, by finding joy in their suffering. It is the ultimate foolishness. Suffering is the last place to look for joy. Nevertheless, the newness of church members' lives is such that they find it. *It* finds *them.*

> With all our affliction, I am overjoyed (2 Cor. 7:4).
>
> We rejoice in our sufferings (Rom. 5:3).
>
> I rejoice in my sufferings for your sake (Col. 1:24).
>
> Even if I am to be poured as a libation upon the sacrificial offering of your faith, I am glad and rejoice with you all (Phil. 2:17).

It was the final reduction. The word "rejoice" meant exult, boast, glory, triumph. Paul triumphed in defeat. He gloried in humility. He boasted in weakness. He exulted in nothingness.

It was the new order. The new life. The new style. It was what he called being "in Christ." They were all to pick it up. "You became imitators of us and of the Lord" (1 Thess. 1:6). "You share in our sufferings . . . [and] our comfort" (2 Cor. 1:7). "You also should be glad and rejoice with me" (Phil. 2:18). And they did. "Count it all joy, my brethren," a later Christian was to write, "when you meet various trials" (James 1:2). "Though now . . . you may have to suffer various trials," wrote another, ". . . you . . . rejoice with unutterable and exalted joy" (1 Pet. 1:6, 8).

Was it naive? Was it gullible? Was it self-deluding? Or was it the *way* to be a church member? It *was* the point then. What has happened now?

NOTES

1. Quoted by F. W. Beare, *The Interpreter's Dictionary of the Bible* (New York: Abingdon, 1962), vol. 3, p. 737.
2. H. Seesemann in Kittel and Friedrich, *Theological Dictionary of the New Testament* (Ann Arbor, Mich.: Eerdmans, 1968), vol. 6, p. 30.
3. Ernest Gordon, *Through the Valley of the Kwai* (New York: Harper & Row, 1962).
4. *V.* also Judg. 2:22, Neh. 9:26, Hos. 6:1.

17

THE POINT IS TO BE A DISCIPLE

The greatest need of the American church is leadership. No other need comes close for urgency, and no other need comes close for difficulty.

It is not that our church leaders do not lead. Surely they are doing their jobs to the best of their abilities. It is that others who should be leading are not. There is a leadership vacuum in our churches. Something must be done to fill it.

The first church members were leaders. Normally we focus on the charisma of Jesus. It is time to remember also the charisma of the disciples. We are in existence as churches today because of their leadership. What was distinctive about it?

I

One, it absorbed them. Their vision of what it meant to lead was total. They lived it, ate it, breathed it, slept it. They *were* their vision.

Now that of course is not new. It is the essence of leadership and always has been. The one who is possessed is the one who leads. The problem is that we do not have enough church people who are possessed.

The church leader cannot be a dilettante. Voting occasionally is not leadership; it is dilettantism. Going to a monthly meeting is not leadership; it is dilettantism. An occasional service of worship is not leadership; it is dilettantism.

The disciple was absorbed by what he was doing. He was in daily contact with his teacher. He learned by example as well as by precept. What is it that, when you do it, you lose all track of time? That is what absorbs you. That is where your discipleship begins.

They knew him.[1] They could not have gone with him if they had not known him. He did not appear out of nowhere. They had been together before. Often. Gradually he absorbed them. Then they went with him.

But that wasn't new. Many left to go with the rabbis. They expounded the Scripture, gathered disciples, walked the land.[2] Then the disciples after a while did the same. They had their disciples, and so on. It was the leadership style of the day. The disciples we know did nothing new.

But this is where it begins. If we are not absorbed by what we are doing, we will never lead it. "If I look at myself objectively," says a Nobel Prize winner, "the first thing I notice is that I find myself running . . . to my laboratory every morning."[3] He is a leader in his field. You can't lead the church if you're going to dabble.

*

But that is not all there is to it. It is not only that we are lost. We are found. There are two sides to absorption, and we may be getting closer to the passive if we remember the second as well as the first. The one thing that Jesus did that *was* new was to issue the call to follow him.[4] *He* took the initiative. The rabbis didn't. The students came to the rabbis; Jesus came to the students. You took your job; as a church leader your job comes to you.

Something, in other words, is coming to us that may absorb us. More to the point, some*one* is coming to us *who* may absorb us.

Dicsipleship, a scholar writes, "always implies the existence of a personal attachment which shapes the whole life of the . . . disciple."[5] There are *no* instances in the New Testament where discipleship is not "supremely personal union."[6] *"I chose you"* (John 15:16).

II

Two, your vision of leadership not only absorbs you, it defies you. It builds you up, but it tears you down. It is you, but it isn't. Any number of people can be absorbed by what they are doing. Fewer can be defied. We may be getting closer to the passive and to the why of the decline of church membership.

"Follow me." But they didn't *want* to follow him. "And I will make you fishers of men." But they wanted to fish for fish. It wasn't their thing. They remonstrated with him to do it their way, not his. They did not understand him. Finally they left him. It was all over. They went back to fishing for fish. "We need leaders," writes John Gardner, "who have stepped out of their special fields to deal with the problems of the total community or . . . nation. And they are in very short supply."[7]

You bet they are. It's one thing to lead my management team; it's another thing to lead my church. It's one thing to lead my assembly line; it's another thing to lead my small group. It's one thing to lead my family; it's another to lead my Bible class.

In every instance the disciples were *totally unqualified* for the job of being disciples. Four of them were businessmen with the largest industry in town. No qualifications except to run a business. Another was a politician. No qualifications except to run a party. Another was a tax collector. No qualifications for anything. He was despised. And the man went into his tax office and said, "Follow me." It defied reason.

But it happened. The least qualified were the most. The ones who couldn't do it could. The fishers of fish were the fishers of men. It made no sense, but there it was. It was as they went up against what defied them that they became real.

The leader goes up against what he is not, in order to become what he is. It makes no sense. Why go up against yourself when you can be absorbed by yourself? Why go on when you could stop? It is only a few who are absorbed by what they are doing. How many? Five percent of the churches? One percent? Why go on to defy yourself? Is it not enough to lead by being caught up in what you are doing? Why go on to what repels you?

*

They failed. It is not only that *we* can't do it. It is that we can't *do* it. It is impossible. It is beyond us. We will fail. Peter denied him. All of them left him. He was as alone at the end as he was at the start. He had come to them, but they would not come to him. "My God, my God, why have you forsaken me?"

It was too big. It defied them. They couldn't *do* it. It was *beyond* their ability. It was not a good plan. It did not make sense. It was not "realistic."

That was the *point.* He gave them a job that *was* too big. He gave them a job for which they were *not* equipped. He *gave* them failure. It was crucial to their development as a church. As before, we failed in Vietnam. It was crucial to our development as people. We draw up plans for churches in order to fail as churches.

"Can't" is the most important word in the Bible. "Follow me." They couldn't follow him. "Turn back." They couldn't turn back. "Repent." They couldn't repent. "Love." They couldn't love. "Obey." They couldn't obey.

It was beyond them. That was the *point*—to give them something as a church that was beyond them. *That* is the point of church membership—to give us what is beyond us, to give us what we can't do, to make us fail. God *is* what makes us fail.

> I am no prophet, nor a prophet's son; but I am a herdsman,
> and a dresser of sycamore trees, and the *Lord* took me from
> following the flock, and the *Lord* said to me, "Go, prophesy
> to my people Israel" (Amos 7:14–15).

It's not your job. You do it. You fail. That *is* God in your life. That is not all God is, but it *is* God. God *is* what absorbs us. God *is* what defies us.

III

Three, God *is* what destroys us. The disciples were beaten. Amos was thrown out of the country. Job was crushed. Moses was leveled. Paul was obliterated by the side of the road. Jeremiah was jailed. Isaiah was mocked. Ezekiel jeered. Jesus killed. All were leaders. The church leader leads by being led.

It is no accident that the highest image in the Bible for church members, as we have seen, is that of the lowest. They were called slaves. Plenty of people followed rabbis around, but no one besides the disciples became a rabbi's slaves. The idea was to follow the rabbi as the first step. Then to become independent of him as the second step. Then to equal or even supersede his teaching as a third step.[8] But that was not the way it was for disciples. Discipleship was the *only* step. Obedience, not independence, was what was demanded.[9] "Slave" was a parallel word for "disciple."[10]

What is a slave? A slave is a person who is not a person. He is destroyed as a person. He has no independent existence of his own. He is totally dependent. *He* is destroyed in order that his master can be built. Everything he does is for his master. He does only what he is told to do.

Jesus ordered his disciples to do two things. And by "disciples" is meant not only the twelve but all who followed him, *all* church members. Ninety percent of the uses of the word "disciple" are not limited to the twelve.[11] "Slaves" and "servants" are the two most frequently used terms in the New Testament for church members.[12] "Every believer," writes an expert, "was considered a slave of God and of Christ."[13]

Jesus told his disciples to do two things. One was "Repent." It was his first sermon. It was his first order to his slaves. It would in turn become their order as leaders. It meant to deny yourself.[14] It meant to renounce yourself. It meant to acknowledge, in other words, your own destruction. That was your death. It was the first step toward your resurrection as a church member.[15]

Now, of course, *we* could not do this.[16] We were so set on leading that we could never be led. We were so set on being "creative," as we say, that we could never be destroyed—by ourselves. God *was* what destroyed us.

The second thing Jesus told his disciples was to "Love." It meant to give yourself. First, you renounce yourself, which is the ultimate affront to a leader. Then you give yourself, which is the ultimate act of a leader. Jesus gave himself; so did the disciples. Legend has it that Peter, too, was crucified, upside down. So are "leading" church members everywhere who advocate, say, that any new building be matched for benevolences. The disciple factor is still at work. So are many people who are not killed, but who give themselves, who allow themselves to become vulnerable, who love.

Now of course *we* cannot do it. It is beyond us. It is a passive act. We can no more give ourselves than we can renounce ourselves. God *is* what enables us to give ourselves. That is not all God is, but God is at least that. "God *is* love," a stunned church member wrote.

So, too, church member, you will go out there. And you will be hurt very much as you lead. And that is as it should be. That is as it must be. They were beaten. They were whipped. They were jailed. They were exiled. Church membership is a demanding vocation.[17]

But something is happening to you as the winds blow and the

waters rise. You who were lost are found. You who were defied are loved. You who were destroyed are born again. You who were a crowd have become a church.

NOTES

1. Frederick C. Grant in *The Interpreter's Bible* (New York: Abingdon, 1951), vol. 7, p. 658; B. Harvie Branscomb in *The Moffatt New Testament Commentary* "Mark" (New York: Harper, n.d.), p. 28; William Barclay, *The Gospel of Mark* (Phila.: Westminster, 1956), p. 20; K. H. Rengstorf in G. Kittel, *Theological Dictionary of the New Testament* (Grand Rapids, Mich.: Eerdmans, 1967), vol. 4, p. 445, 458.

2. Rengstorf. *op. cit.,* p. 449.

3. Albert Szent-Gyorgi, *New York Times Magazine,* 30 July 1961.

4. Rengstorf, *op. cit.,* p. 444.

5. *Ibid.,* p. 441.

6. *Ibid.,* p. 442.

7. John Gardner, quoted in *Christian Science Monitor,* 16 April 1969.

8. Rengstorf, *op. cit.,* p. 448.

9. *Ibid.,* p. 449.

10. *Ibid.,* p. 448.

11. Pierson Parker in *The Interpreter's Dictionary of the Bible* (New York: Abingdon, 1962), vol. 4, p. 34.

12. P. S. Minear in *The Interpreter's Dictionary of the Bible* (New York: Abingdon, 1962), vol. 1, p. 610.

13. *Idem.*

14. "If any man would come after me, let him deny himself" (Luke 9:23).

15. 2 Cor. 5:17.

16. W. A. Quanbeck in *The Interpreter's Dictionary of the Bible* (New York: Abingdon, 1962), vol. 4, p. 34.

17. "Whoever does not bear his own cross and come after me, cannot be my disciple" (Luke 14:27).